D1260454

MEDORA COMM. SCHOOL LIBRARY

IMAGES ACROSS THE AGES

AFRICAN PORTRAITS

Dorothy
and
Thomas Hoobler

RSVP
**RAINTREE
STECK-VAUGHN**
P U B L I S H E R S
The Steck-Vaughn Company

Austin, Texas

MEDORA COMM. SCHOOL LIBRARY

Copyright © 1993 Steck-Vaughn Company

All rights reserved. No part of this book may be reproduced or utilized in any form or by any means, electronic or mechanical, including photocopying, recording, or by any information storage and retrieval system, without permission in writing from the Publisher. Inquiries should be addressed to Steck-Vaughn, P.O. Box 26015, Austin, TX 78755.

Cover and interior design: Suzanne Beck
Illustrations: John Gampert, Represented by Creative Freelancers
Electronic Production: Scott Melcer
Project Manager: Joyce Spicer

Library of Congress Cataloging-in-Publication Data
Hoobler, Dorothy.
    African portraits / by Dorothy and Thomas Hoobler: illustrated by John Gampert
      p.   cm. — (Images across the ages)
    Includes bibliographical references and index.
    Summary: Presents biographies of some prominent sub-Saharan African people throughout history, including Piankhy, Ahmed Baba, Ann Nzinga, Cinque, Kip Keino, and Wole Soyinka.
    ISBN 0-8114-6378-8
    1. Africa, Sub-Saharan — Biography — Juvenile literature.
[1. Africa, Sub-Saharan — Biography.]   I. Hoobler, Thomas.
II. Gampert, John, ill.   III. Title.   IV. Series : Hoobler, Dorothy.
Images across the ages.
    CT1920.H66   1993
    920.067—dc20   92-17284
                                                          CIP AC

Printed and bound in the United States by Lake Book, Melrose Park, IL
  2 3 4 5 6 7 8 9 0 LB 98 97 96 95 94

Acknowledgments
Excerpt from "Live Burial" from *A Shuttle in the Crypt* by Wole Soyinka. Copyright © 1972 by Wole Soyinka. Reprinted by permission of Hill and Wang, a division of Farrar, Straus & Giroux, Inc.
Our thanks to Robert W. July for his generous help and advice.

CONTENTS

INTRODUCTION: THE HOMELAND OF HUMANKIND 4

1 THE CONQUEROR OF EGYPT—PIANKHY 6

2 CHRISTIANITY COMES TO ETHIOPIA—
   EZANA AND LALIBELA 13

3 "THE RICHEST AND MOST NOBLE KING"—
   MANSA MUSA 19

4 THE PEARL OF HIS TIME—AHMED BABA 25

5 BRASS THAT REMEMBERS—EUWARE THE GREAT 32

6 THE WARRIOR QUEEN—ANN NZINGA 38

7 "GIVE US FREE"—CINQUE 45

8 "THE BEGINNING OF A NEW DAY"—
   MENELIK II AND TAITU 52

9 "SELF-GOVERNMENT NOW"—KWAME NKRUMAH 59

10 A WRITER FROM TWO WORLDS—WOLE SOYINKA 69

11 THE RUNNING POLICEMAN—KIPCHOGE KEINO 75

12 "MUSIC IS A TYPE OF MAGIC"—
   MIRIAM MAKEBA AND JOSEPH SHABALALA 81

Glossary 89

Bibliography 91

Sources 93

Index 95

MEDORA COMM SCHOOL LIBRARY

THE HOMELAND OF HUMANKIND

Call her Eve. A group of scientists recently declared that all of the 5.4 billion human beings now living in the world have a single ancestor—a woman who lived in Africa around 200,000 years ago.

Scientists at the University of California took samples of body tissue from many different racial and ethnic groups all over the world. Laboratory workers studied the DNA, the material in human cells that transmits characteristics from one generation to the next. Using computers to correlate the thousands of bits of information in each cell, the scientists created a human "family tree." It led back to what the California researchers believe is the mother of the human race.

Not all scientists agree with the "Eve" theory. Some think that *Homo sapiens* ("Wise Man"), the modern form of human beings, developed in several different locations around the world. All scientists, however, accept that the "granddaddy" of modern humans, an earlier type called *Homo habilis* ("Handy Man"), first appeared in Africa.

That discovery was made by Louis and Mary Leakey in 1959 in Olduvai Gorge in the nation of Kenya. There, the two anthropologists unearthed the fossil remains of a creature that lived around 1.8 million years ago. Casts made of the inside of its skull showed that its brain was larger than that of its apelike relatives; a bulge in one part of the brain indicated that it probably used a form of spoken language. Nearby, the Leakeys found stone tools that this creature or its relatives had made, giving it the Latin name that means "handy man." A later discovery, also in Kenya, showed that "handy man" probably existed at least 2.4 million years ago.

Over more than two million years, descendants of "handy man" spread throughout the world. Many of them, of course, remained in Africa. Some lived in the area where the Sahara Desert is now. Cave paintings show that as recently as 6,000 years ago, the desert region was very different from what it is today. In fact, it had a wet climate. Heavy rainfall produced rivers and large, shallow lakes. The region was covered by fertile grasslands and forests in which giraffes, rhinoceroses, and elephants lived. The rivers provided a habitat for fish and crocodiles. The environment supported a good life for the human fishers and hunters who formed settlements there.

Then the climate started to change. The rains came less and less often, and the region became hotter and drier. As the rivers and lakes evaporated, the large animals retreated south. The human beings in the area survived by gathering root crops. Eventually their food supply became so sparse that most of the people also moved southward to find more favorable living conditions.

By 2000 B.C. the desert had become the largest in the world. The Arabs gave it the name *Sahra*, meaning "wilderness." To the Arabs, the word *Sahra* imitated the sound of a thirsty person gasping for water.

As the desert spread, it drew a great dividing line across the continent. The civilizations to the north were linked to the other societies around the Mediterranean Sea. Though a few traders traveled across the Sahara, the desert tended to cut off the African civilizations to the south from the rest of the world. Thus, African societies south of the Sahara developed unique cultures and traditions. It is these people, in sub-Saharan Africa, who are the subjects of this book.

CHAPTER 1

THE CONQUERER OF EGYPT—
PIANKHY

Around the year 741 B.C., Piankhy, the King of Kush, looked with pride on the mighty army he had assembled. A line of boats, ready to carry his warriors northward, stretched for miles along the Nile River. This immense force was about to embark on one of the boldest ventures of ancient times—the conquest of Egypt.

The people of Kush, in today's country of Sudan, had been dominated by Egypt for nearly 2,000 years. During that time, Egypt had sent its soldiers up the Nile River, which begins deep within Africa and flows from south to north. When the Egyptians reached Kush, they demanded tribute from its people, taking some of them away as slaves. Year after year the Egyptians returned. Over time, they built forts along the Nile to control their southern neighbors.

Piankhy set out to change all that. At first his generals sent him news of victory after victory. However, the Kushite army became stalled at Hermopolis, one of the fortress-cities that secured Egypt's control of the Nile.

Impatient, Piankhy went there to look over the situation, bringing his wives and sisters along. The city's ruler, Namlot, relied on its strong walls to keep the enemy out. Piankhy began a siege, keeping food and supplies from entering Hermopolis. Namlot sent messengers with gifts to Piankhy, trying to persuade him to leave. But Piankhy would not budge.

At last Namlot could hold out no longer. However, he feared Piankhy's wrath, and sent his queen to plead with the women of Piankhy's court. Piankhy's heart was moved. He promised to spare Namlot and the people of the city. The gates were opened.

Piankhy later built a granite column on which he inscribed the story of his conquests. He wrote there: "Hermopolis threw herself upon her belly and pleaded before the king [Piankhy]. Messengers

came forth...bearing everything beautiful to behold; gold, every splendid costly stone, clothing...." For days, the city's people spread their treasures before the king of Kush.

Namlot declared himself to be Piankhy's slave and placed his own headdress on Piankhy's head. On the top of the headdress was the *uraeus*, or coiled snake, that was the symbol of the power of Egypt's pharaoh.

That was fitting, for Piankhy was not content with the conquest of Hermopolis. He intended to make himself ruler of all Egypt.

Kush was the earliest African kingdom south of Egypt. The legendary Greek poet Homer wrote about the Kushites in the *Iliad*, saying they lived at the end of the world. According to Homer, gods attended their banquets and when the sun set, it rested on their country.

Piankhy, or Piye as he is sometimes known, was born in Napata, the capital of Kush. As one of the sons of the royal family, he was regarded as partly divine. According to the Kushite religion, Amon, the god of the sun, was the true father of the royal children. It worked this way. Amon visited the queen disguised as her husband and she became pregnant. When Piankhy was born, his mother presented him to the king not as his baby but as the child of Amon.

Napata was a beautiful city. Piankhy grew up in a large palace made of mud bricks. The common people lived in wooden huts topped with cone-shaped grass roofs. The people grew millet and kept cattle in nearby fields. Through the city walked the proud warriors of Kush in leopard-skin skirts, wearing splendid jewelry in their ears and around their necks.

Young Piankhy trained for his future role as king. He practiced with his bow and arrow and learned the tactics of warfare. He also learned the sacred lore of the gods, and mastered the complicated hieroglyphic writing that Kush had borrowed from the Egyptians.

The people of Napata were proud of their devotion to the gods. The holiest shrine of all lay to the south of the city. Still there today, it is a reddish sandstone butte that juts up from the flat sandy plain, visible for miles around. The people of Kush called it the Hill of Barkal. They believed it to be a holy place where Amon, the most important god in Egyptian mythology lived. Guarding the hill were stone statues of rams, male sheep, the symbol of Amon.

8

The statues of Amon showed him with the horned head of a ram.

The priests of Amon in Napata believed that they practiced a purer form of the religion than their neighbor to the north—Egypt. Over many centuries, the Egyptian religion had developed new forms of worship, while the Kushites kept the ancient ways.

Piankhy often thought about the relationship between the two countries. Because Egypt had conquered Kush, the Egyptians hated and feared what they called "miserable Kush." Egyptian wall paintings show the black-skinned Kushites bound as slaves. One pharaoh, Tutankhamen, had pictures of Kushites painted on the soles of his sandals, so that he could trample on them daily. (This was the same "King Tut" whose tomb was uncovered in the twentieth century; among the objects found within it were those same sandals.)

Kush had been forced to pay tribute to Egypt through an unfair form of trade. In exchange for grain from Egypt, Kush sent gold from the desert mines near Napata, animal skins, elephant tusks, and carnelian (a stone that was used for arrowheads and jewelry.) Egypt took its tribute in slaves as well. Kushite slaves worked in the households of wealthy Egyptians or served in the pharaoh's army. The warriors of Kush were famous for their skill with bow and arrows.

From an early age, Piankhy believed his destiny was to free his people from Egypt's dominance. On the stone tablet that describes his conquests, Piankhy told of hearing the god Amon speak to him:

> While you were yet in the body of your mother, I ordained that you would be ruler of Egypt. I knew you in the seed while you were in the egg, that you were to be Lord....A father makes excellent his son, and I am he who has decreed the kingship for you.

While Piankhy was growing up, Egypt was in a period of decline. The ruler of Kush, King Kashta, took advantage of this weakness to conquer parts of southern Egypt. Piankhy planned to go farther. After Kashta's death, the priests of Amon chose Piankhy to be his successor. He was invested with the sacred regalia of his office. He was given a crown with two golden cobras twining around it, topped with very tall feathers. The priests placed on his thumb a large gold ring with an all-seeing eye etched upon it. Kushite warriors wore a thumb ring to help them pull their bowstrings.

Although he was king, Piankhy did not rule alone. He followed the advice and counsel of the priests of Amon. By listening to a statue of the god, the priests received Amon's wishes and passed them on to the king. Indeed, Amon had spoken in this way to choose which one of Kashta's sons would succeed him.

Piankhy, in turn, reported his dreams to priests who were trained in interpreting them. When he told them that Amon had spoken to him, the priests' advice matched Piankhy's desires: it was time to invade Egypt.

Piankhy was only twenty-one years old when he loaded his ships with warriors. From his capital he sent orders to his commanders:

> Do not stop by day or night; do not sit thinking as at a game...but fight at sight. Force battle on the enemy from far off; force it first on the pick of his troops....for you know that Amon is God, and that it is He who has sent us.

After taking Hermopolis, Piankhy swept down the Nile "like a cloudburst." On he went, sweeping all resistance aside. Finally he reached Memphis, Egypt's capital city, more than 1,200 miles down the Nile from Napata. If Memphis fell, Piankhy would control virtually all of Egypt.

News of Piankhy's victories had reached the city, but the Egyptians felt confident. Memphis too was protected by a high wall, and its defenders had gathered a stock of food large enough to last through a long siege.

Memphis stood on the west bank of the Nile. The wall was highest on the western side, facing the land, because in the past, invaders had come from that direction. The wall along the river was not so high, because it was thought impossible for soldiers to scale it from the water. Most of the Egyptian soldiers were guarding the western wall.

Piankhy foiled them with brilliant military tactics. His boats swept into the city's harbor and captured the Egyptian fleet. Piankhy lined up his boats at the base of the seawall to provide a foothold for his soldiers. They swarmed to the top of the wall so swiftly that the Egyptians could not bring up their main forces in time to stop them. Once inside the city, the skilled Kushite archers mowed down the Egyptians. The richest city in Egypt was now in Piankhy's hands.

He had one final goal: Heliopolis, "city of the sun," where the reigning pharaoh lived under the protection of Amon, the sun god. By the time Piankhy appeared, all resistance had dissolved. The pharaoh and fifteen of his lords humbly surrendered.

Piankhy marched to the temple of Amon. Because the priests knew that he was now their master, they opened its doors. They took him to a sacred chamber and dressed him in the pharaoh's garments. They purified Piankhy's body with incense and holy liquids, bringing him flowers and garlands from the "pyramidon-house," the place where Amon lived.

Now Piankhy was prepared to visit the pyramidon-house.

With his own hands, he broke open the bolts of its two great doors and opened them. Alone with the god, he offered a prayer of thanksgiving. Then he shut the doors again, setting his own clay seals on them. He told the priests: "I have [made] the seal. No other shall enter therein of all the kings who shall arise."

Because Piankhy had entered the god's chamber and survived, the priests "threw themselves on their bellies before his majesty" and declared that he would live forever. Piankhy proclaimed himself ruler of Egypt and founded the twenty-fifth dynasty, or ruling

family, of that ancient country. His descendants would continue to rule after his death.

Piankhy sailed back to Napata with ships laden with booty—silver, gold, copper, fine woods, and clothing. He used them to beautify his capital, Napata. One of his greatest projects was a huge temple to honor Amon. Its ruins have been found on the Hill of Barkal. Within was the pillar that describes his victories, beginning: "Listen to what I did!—I who am...the living image of the sun-god destined to rule from birth."

Piankhy proclaimed Amon the supreme god and appointed new rulers of the regions under his control. As the pillar says: "He to whom I say, 'thou art a king' shall be a king; he to whom I say, 'thou shalt not be a king' shall not be a king." He employed artists to decorate temples with the styles of sculpture and painting used a thousand years before, because that was the time when Amon was properly worshiped. Many of the Kushites' wall paintings do in fact look very much like those of ancient Egypt.

Following Kushite custom, Piankhy had many wives. The one he may have loved most was named Nefru-ka-Kashta. A figurine from that time shows her suckling at the breast of a goddess. Usually, only kings were honored in this way.

When Piankhy died, his body was interred in an underground chamber filled with treasures and statues of servants. Like the Egyptians, the Kushites built a pyramid to mark the spot, though the Egyptians put their burial chambers within the pyramid, not underneath it.

Piankhy's son Shabaka took his father's place, ruling an empire that stretched from the Mediterranean Sea to the juncture of the Blue and White Niles. The Kushite Dynasty ruled Egypt for more than sixty years. Then Assyrians from Asia conquered Egypt, but the kingdom of Kush survived.

Around 590 B.C. the Kushite kings moved their capital farther south to Meroe. From here, Piankhy's descendants ruled for another 800 years, but the kings still went to the temple at Napata to be crowned. The Kushites carried on trade with countries from India to the Roman Empire. At Meroe, they developed their own writing script. Because no one today can decipher it, the civilization of Kush still holds many mysteries. Nevertheless, the name and deeds of Piankhy have survived for nearly 2,700 years.

C H A P T E R 2

CHRISTIANITY COMES TO ETHIOPIA—EZANA AND LALIBELA

Early in the fourth century A.D., a ship loaded with trade goods sailed down the Red Sea, bound for India. On board were two young Syrians named Frumentius and Aedesius, traveling with their uncle. Suddenly pirates attacked the ship. They swarmed over the sides and slaughtered the crew. The two young men saw their uncle murdered before their eyes. Frumentius and Aedisius were spared, and after a series of adventures came ashore at Adulis on the northeast coast of Africa.

Adulis was a busy port city, the trading center of the kingdom of Axum (today's Ethiopia.) Foreign traders brought their wares to Adulis to trade for ivory, the main export of the country. They also desired the fine crystal glass and brass or copper jewelry made by the craftspeople of Adulis. Precious woods, fragrances, and incense were for sale. Among the perfumes were frankincense and myrrh, gifts that the three kings brought to the new-born Christ.

The golden coins of Axum, imprinted with moon and stars, were recognized and accepted throughout the coastal towns of the Mediterranean Sea and the Indian Ocean. Through the dusty streets of Adulis walked merchants from Egypt, India, Greece, and Rome. In its markets, people could buy Chinese silk, cotton cloth and spices from India, and olive oil and wine from the Mediterranean countries. Gold and silver from many nations changed hands there.

Frumentius and Aedisius left Adulis and traveled inland. After a journey of eight days, they reached the capital city, called Axum. They saw an amazing sight—very tall, thin stone monuments that rose high above the city's houses. More than one hundred of these obelisks decorated Axum. Some are still standing today. Richly decorated with unusual designs, each one was carved from a single block of stone. The largest was 110 feet high, taller

than any pillar ever built from one piece of stone. Those who saw these skinny skyscrapers thought they were among the wonders of the ancient world. What their purpose may have been is still a mystery. They may have been celebrations of great battles or monuments to the dead.

The two Syrians met the king, Ella Amida, who was impressed by their learning. He appointed Frumentius treasurer of the kingdom and made Aedisius his cupbearer, an honored position. Frumentius' influence on the king's son, Ezana, brought changes to Axum that are still felt in Ethiopia today.

King Ella Amida was a member of the Solomonid Dynasty, which proudly traced its lineage back to Biblical times. Their early homeland, called Saba, was located in Yemen in southern Arabia. One of Saba's ancient rulers, the Queen of Saba (Sheba), is mentioned in the Bible. She brought fabulous gifts of gold and spices to King Solomon. In Ethiopian tradition, the Queen of Saba and King Solomon had a child, named Menelik, who became the first king of Axum.

Sometime before 500 B.C., immigrants from Saba arrived on the African coast and intermarried with the Africans. The Sabaite immigrants brought with them a written language, highly developed skills in building, and the use of irrigation in agriculture. All these helped the people of Axum to flourish.

The Axumites also followed the old religion of Saba. They worshiped the stars and other heavenly bodies, particularly the planet Venus. That was why the coins of Axum showed the moon and stars. Ezana grew up in the ancient faith, but when Frumentius came to the court, he began to teach the boy about Christianity, Frumentius' own faith. Christian merchants had visited Adulis before, but they had made no attempt to spread their religion.

Frumentius's teachings impressed the young prince. After Ezana became king around the A.D. 320, he converted to Christianity and made it the official religion of Axum. He changed the coins—now they had a cross on the back and his portrait on the front.

Frumentius traveled to Egypt to report the good news to the archbishop of Alexandria. The archbishop named Frumentius the first bishop of Axum and sent him back to guide the church. Ezana enthusiastically began to build Christian churches throughout his domain. A lasting bond was created between Christianity and the state of Ethiopia.

Travelers were awed by the splendors of the court of Axum. The towers of King Ezana's palace were topped by statues of unicorns. Giraffes and elephants roamed in the courtyard and were treated as household pets. The people of the city bowed before their king when he traveled forth in his four-wheeled, golden chariot drawn by four elephants. On public occasions, the king wore a linen gown embroidered with gold and a turban topped with gold, pearls, and precious stones.

The main source of Ezana's wealth and power came from the trade at Adulis. He received taxes on all imports and exports. Because of the importance of this trade, Ezana took steps to protect it. Sometimes bandits waylaid caravans bringing ivory, rhinoceros horn, and gold from the south. Ezana sent soldiers to wipe out the bandit gangs. In doing so, he gradually expanded the territory under his domain, demanding tribute from neighboring rulers.

Ezana came into conflict with the kingdom of Meroe, still ruled by Piankhy's descendants. The messengers that Ezana sent to them were stripped and humiliated. Sometime around 350, Ezana conquered the once-flourishing city. He commemorated his victory on a pillar at Axum:

> And as I have sent warnings to them, and they would not listen to me...and heaped insults upon me...I made war upon them....I burnt their towns...and my soldiers carried off their food, as well as copper, iron, and brass...destroyed the statues in their

temples...and their cotton trees, casting them into the River Seda [Nile].

Under Ezana's successors, the great empire of Axum continued to grow and flourish for more than four centuries. Then it was invaded by Islamic warriors. In the seventh century A.D., Muhammad, a merchant in the Arabian city of Mecca, had founded a new religion, called Islam. After Muhammad's death, his militant followers spread their faith in a series of rapid conquests. Sailing across the Red Sea, the Islamic warriors captured the city of Adulis, cutting off the kings of Axum from the source of their wealth.

Though isolated from the coast, the people of Axum gradually spread their influence and their Christian religion into the mountains and highlands to the south.

Around the twelfth century, a new Ethiopian dynasty, called the Zagwe, seized power. By now, the kingdom was centered in the Lasta Mountains far to the south of Axum. The Zagwe court was located at Roha, a town close to Ras Dashen, the highest peak in the country. In the highlands the Ethiopians had remained faithful to Christianity, adding their own rites and traditions over the years.

The most famous Zagwe king was King Lalibela. As a youth, Lalibela was very pious, performing his religious duties with great fervor. According to legend, when Lalibela became king he was transported to heaven. God commanded him to build churches for the Christians of Ethiopia. Returning to earth, Lalibela set out to recreate his idea of the holy city of Jerusalem.

The churches he built are some of the world's most unusual structures. The city of Roha was surrounded by mammoth rock formations. Lalibela ordered his craftsmen to build churches out of them—not by breaking the rock into blocks, but by carving each massive stone into a single structure.

It was a mammoth task, but Lalibela's work force included angels sent by God. Since they did not need to sleep, they worked around the clock. An Ethiopian chronicle says the human workers

> would do a cubit's work during the day, but would find a further three cubits completed on the morrow....They doubted whether the angels were doing this work because they could not see them, but Lalibela knew, because the angels, who understood his virtue, did not hide from him.

Whether or not angels really helped, the eleven churches Lalibela built still exist today. It is clear that an awesome amount of work was required to complete them. The workers carved the surrounding rock away until the exterior of the church was completed. Then they made windows and doorways and carved out the interior. Painters decorated the walls with scenes from the Bible and Ethiopian history.

The Zagwe were apparently familiar with many styles of architecture, for each church is different. Some show the influence of the Romans; others are like Byzantine Christian churches. Modern experts have even found traces of Persian and Chinese influences. It is a shame we do not know the names of the architects of these wonderful churches.

The largest church, named The Redeemer of the World, is more than 100 feet long and 70 feet wide. Its upper windows, shaped like the tall obelisks of Axum, allow only a pale light to filter into the dim interior. But the windows were placed so that at certain times of day, the sun falls on the high altar.

Another church, dedicated to Saint George, is shaped like a Greek cross, with four arms of equal length. Legends say that it was built on the command of Saint George himself. When the saint saw that no church had been erected in his honor, he came galloping into Roha to demand one. A stone near the church bears the hoofprint of Saint George's horse.

The most sacred spot of Ethiopian Christianity is a crypt beneath the Church of Golgotha-Mikael. Three high stone altars rise from the floor; on the center one is a carving of Saint Matthew, one of the writers of the Gospels. Even today, priests of Ethiopian Christianity descend to the dark chamber, lit only by candles, to perform the most sacred rites of their religion.

After the churches were completed, Lalibela abdicated his throne. He spent the rest of his life as a hermit, sleeping on rocks and eating roots and herbs. After his death, he was buried in the Church of Golgotha-Mikael, but he was never forgotten. The city of Roha was renamed Lalibela, and is popularly called the "Jerusalem of Ethiopia." The churches still attract worshipers from all over Ethiopia, who honor Lalibela as a saint.

C H A P T E R 3

"THE RICHEST AND MOST NOBLE KING"—MANSA MUSA

In the year 1324 Musa, the *mansa*, or emperor, of the West African empire of Mali, knelt in prayer. He was about to leave his capital city, Niane, located on the upper part of the Niger River. As Mansa Musa prayed for a safe journey, he faced northeast. In that direction lay Mecca, the holy city of Islam that Muslims all over the world turn to when they say their daily prayers.

Mansa Musa, a devout follower of Islam, was about to perform a duty required of all Muslims once in their lifetimes. He was making the *hajj*, or pilgrimage, to Mecca, the city of Muhammad's birth. An enormous caravan of camels waited for Mansa Musa to give the signal to start. On his journey he would be accompanied by 60,000 of his subjects. To make sure they would be welcomed wherever they traveled, the caravan included eighty camels—each carrying 300 pounds of gold dust. His bodyguards' spears and swords were tipped with gold that glinted in the rays of the sun.

The first part of the journey would be the hardest—crossing the burning sands of the Sahara Desert. All the trappings of kingship could not ease the hardships of the two-month journey. The caravan had able guides who could steer the way over the barren wastes. Taking a wrong turn could be fatal, for supplies of water were scarce and reaching the closest oasis was always necessary.

At every small stream that marked an oasis, Mansa Musa generously rewarded the people who lived around it. For a caravan of this size was not often seen. Even so, as he lay down to rest in his magnificent tent, nothing could protect him from desert lice and scorpions. And if a strong wind blew, desert sandstorms could wipe out the subtle landmarks by which the guides navigated.

The Mansa warned his guards to keep an eye out for brigands, especially the Tuareg people who often preyed on travelers.

Fearsome fighters, the Tuaregs could suddenly appear from behind a high dune, showing no mercy to their victims. The Tuaregs, riding camels, presented a striking appearance in their desert garb. They dressed in loose garments to protect themselves from the sun, and enclosed their faces in a *litham*, a blue cotton mask with only narrow slits for the eyes. Often they would seize caravan goods and escape by doubling back to hide their tracks. They were ferocious fighters, and no one knew the Sahara as well as they did.

Mansa Musa avoided danger and arrived safely at Sjilmasa in today's southern Morocco. From here the rest of the year-long trip would not be so arduous. His fabled pilgrimage to Mecca would bring Mansa Musa lasting fame and glory.

The grand caravan of Mali's emperor was not the first to cross the desert that separated the northern coast of Africa from the lands farther south. For centuries, ambitious traders from North Africa had brought fine cloth, glass beads, tempered steel, copper, cowrie shells, and slaves across the Sahara. On the southern edge of the desert, these traders exchanged their goods for leather, slaves, acacia gum, cotton cloths, and—most importantly—gold.

In ancient times few people were hardy or brave enough to make the journey across the desert. But around the time of Christ's birth, camels from Arabia were imported to north Africa. From that time, the trans-Sahara trade increased, bringing wealth and power to those who controlled it. The result was the growth of several great African empires. After crossing the Sahara, traders from the north met people who lived in villages located in today's countries of Mali, Mauritania, and Guinea. The villagers organized to protect their end of the trade, and over time combined into an empire called Ghana. (Not to be confused with the modern nation of Ghana, which lies farther east.)

The people of Ghana obtained gold from sources farther to the south. They used it to trade for cloth and salt, which was much in demand for its use in preserving food. Neither the northern traders nor the people of Ghana could speak each other's language—nor did they trust each other. They exchanged goods in a process called "the silent trade."

When traders from the north reached the boundary of Ghana, they beat drums to announce their arrival. Then they placed their wares on the ground and withdrew. The people of Ghana appeared and set a quantity of gold next to the goods. They too moved out of sight. The traders came back to see how much gold had been left. If they thought it was a fair price, they beat their drums and took it. If not, they left it on the ground. The people of Ghana had their choice of increasing the gold or deciding not to trade.

The capital of Ghana, Kumbi Saleh, became a rich and prosperous city. An Arab traveler of the eleventh century wrote that the emperor held court in a domed pavilion, around which stood ten horses outfitted with gold trappings. On guard at the door were dogs wearing collars of gold and silver. When the emperor received his ministers and subjects, his people approached him on their knees, sprinkling dust on their heads as a sign of respect.

In the year 1076 Muslim warriors from Morocco attempted to conquer the empire of Ghana, but met fierce resistance. However, the invasion disrupted the trade and weakened Ghana, which then broke up into smaller kingdoms.

A century and a half later another leader appeared, named Sundiata. We know about him through the *griots*, or oral historians, who passed down the stories of their kings from generation to generation. According to one legend, Sundiata was born with a withered leg, but overcame his handicap to become a great warrior. His people, the Kangaba, had been conquered by their neighbors, the Sasso. But Sundiata assembled an army to overthrow the Sasso king. Legend also says that he gained his final victory by using a magic potion that the magicians of Sasso could not overcome.

Sundiata persuaded other rulers to join a new empire, called Mali. It eventually became more than twice the size of Ghana. Sundiata brought under his control the gold mines in the forests that lay to the south of old Ghana. These provided the fabulous wealth that made Mali a great trading power. Muslim traders again appeared from beyond the Sahara and converted some of Sundiata's descendants to their religion, Islam.

One of these descendants was Sundiata's grand-nephew, Mansa Musa. He ruled Mali from 1312 to 1337, when it was at the very height of its power. Musa controlled an empire that extended from the Atlantic Ocean eastward past the great bend of the Niger River—an area about the size of western Europe.

When Musa made the holy pilgrimage to Mecca, he revealed

to the world just how rich his empire was. He gave so many presents and spent so freely—always paying in gold—that his name became known even in Europe. Fifty years later, Abraham Cresque, a Jewish mapmaker from the island of Majorca, made an atlas of the world known as the Catalan Atlas. Cresque drew on the map of Africa a picture of Mansa Musa, dressed like a European king and holding a nugget of gold in his hand. The mapmaker wrote that Musa was "the richest and most noble king in all the land."

When Musa's caravan passed through Cairo, Egypt, he gave alms to the poor and lavish presents to those who met him. A chronicler described his effect on the city:

> This man spread upon Cairo the flood of his generosity: there was no person, officer of the court or holder of any office of the sultanate who did not receive a sum in gold from him. The people of Cairo earned incalcuable sums from him, whether by buying or selling or by gifts.

The trip had an effect on Musa and his empire as well. At Mecca he met scholars, poets, and architects from throughout the Muslim world. Muslim doctors and scientists were among the world's best. With his endless supply of gold, Musa persuaded some of the Muslim scholars and scientists to accompany him home to open schools and mosques throughout his domain.

Although Mansa Musa and some of his officials were Muslims, most of his subjects were not. They worshiped ancestors and the "spirits of the land" who ensured a good harvest. Musa had tried to convert them to Islam but with little success. When he sent a Muslim to teach the gold miners, they threatened to stop working if they were forced to convert to Islam.

Musa decided not to anger his subjects. He allowed them to continue their own forms of worship. However, he did establish a school of Muslim studies at the city of Timbuktu. In later centuries it would become a great African university.

During Musa's trip to Mecca, his faithful army had continued his conquests. They captured the city of Gao, the capital of the Songhay people. On his return, Musa visited Gao and took two of the Songhay princes back to his own capital as hostages. He treated them as members of his own family.

Mansa Musa was a ruler of vision who governed his kingdom with fairness and justice. Farmers grew abundant crops to support the huge empire. The fiber of cotton plants was used to produce cloth that was dyed in different colors. Many craftspeople could be found in the cities, and trade was brisk between all the parts of the great empire. Traders from the north noted that few people suffered from poverty.

A few decades after Musa's death, the great Arab traveler Ibn Battuta passed through Mali. He had seen most of the lands under Muslim control and had traveled as far as China. Yet he found much to praise in Mali:

> The small number of acts of injustice that one finds there; for the Negroes are of all peoples those who most abhor injustice. The sultan pardons no one who is guilty of it.

> The complete and general safety one enjoys throughout the land. The traveler has no more reason than the man who stays at home to fear brigands, thieves or rapists....

> On Fridays, anyone who is late at the mosque will find nowhere to pray, the crowd is so great.

> They zealously learn the Koran by heart. Those children who are neglectful in this are put in chains until they have memorized the Koran.

After Musa's death, his brother Suleiman took the throne. Ibn Battuta reported that Suleiman was not as generous as his brother, and that Suleiman's wife led an unsuccessful attempt to overthrow him. The two Songhay princes that Musa had taken as hostages escaped. Not long after Suleiman's death, the Songhay people rose up in revolt against Mali. A new great West African empire was beginning.

C H A P T E R 4

"THE PEARL OF HIS TIME"—
AHMED BABA

Timbuktu! For centuries, the name was repeated in story and legend. People in the Muslim world and in Europe had heard tales of the caravans loaded with gold that passed through the fabulous city somewhere in the Sahara Desert. It was said that Africans had built a university there, whose scholars rivaled any in the world. Five times a day the city resounded with the cries of *muezzins* (prayerleaders) calling the people to their religious duties—just as they did in Cairo, in Baghdad, and in Mecca itself. A garbled form of the name Timbuktu appeared on the Catalan Atlas drawn in 1375. Yet who could tell if such a city really existed? No European had ever crossed the desert to see it.

So in the year 1520, Pope Leo X listened raptly to the stories of a man who had visited Timbuktu. This man, a Muslim, had been captured by Christian pirates. Taken to Rome, he converted to Christianity, taking the name Leo Africanus ("Leo the African") in honor of the pope.

Leo Africanus confirmed all the rumors of the fabled city. He described it as being located in a region that abounded in "corn, cattle, milk, and butter." Within the city lived many "doctors, judges, priests, and other learned men." The king of the region paid them lavish salaries for their services, and the city abounded in wealth. Its people used coins of pure gold, without any markings. For smaller purchases they exchanged valuable shells brought from the kingdom of Persia. More precious than shells or gold, however, were the manuscripts and books imported from the Muslim sultanates in North Africa. These books, Leo Africanus told the pope, "are sold for more money than any other merchandise." For the people prized learning above all else.

The inhabitants of Timbuktu, Leo said, were "people of gentle and cheerful disposition, and spend a great part of the night singing and dancing through all the streets of the city."

Yes, Timbuktu was a real city. In the century following Leo Africanus' account of it, Ahmed Baba, one of the greatest of its scholars, taught at the university there. Ahmed was so well known for his wisdom and learning that he was called "The Unique Pearl of His Time."

Ahmed Baba was born in 1556 at Arawan, a part of the Songhay Empire that had arisen as the empire of Mali declined. Sunni Ali, one of the two Songhay princes that Mansa Musa had taken hostage, never forgot the humiliation his people had suffered. When he escaped from captivity, he assembled an army to take back the Songhay lands. He recaptured the city of Gao, which he made the capital of his new empire. Over time, he conquered Mali and extended his domains farther to the east.

Sunni Ali was ruthless not only toward his enemies, but even to those closest to him. However, his courtiers knew that his temper quickly cooled. Once he ordered a secretary, who had dared to argue with him, put to death. Later, when Sunni Ali received a book in a language no one could read, he regretted that his learned secretary was dead. The courtiers, however, brought out the secretary, who had only been imprisoned in case he was needed.

According to one account, one of Sunni Ali's best generals was spared in a similar manner. This was fortunate for Songhay, for this general, named Muhammad ben Abu Bekr, guided the empire to the height of its glory.

When Sunni Ali died, his son became king. But the son was too weak to rule in his father's place, and fighting soon broke out among those who wished to overthrow him. General Muhammad used his military skill to put down all opposition—but then took the throne for himself.

One of Sunni Ali's daughters taunted Muhammad, calling him *askia*, which means "thief." Muhammad wryly took Askia as his title, perhaps to remind others that he ruled not by inheritance, but because he was powerful. Later historians have called him Askia the Great, for his reign was a glorious time of prosperity for the Songhay Empire. It was on a mission to Askia Muhammad that Leo Africanus had seen Timbuktu.

However, Askia Muhammad was more than just a powerful general. He was a wily diplomat who arranged marriages between his family and local kings within his empire to ensure their loyalty. He organized the empire into provinces and placed a trusted viceroy in charge of each one. To enforce his rule, Askia Muhammad recruited soldiers from all over the empire and beyond. His army included mounted horsemen from Africa's northern coasts. They traveled so swiftly on their horses that it was said they moved "like a cloud of grasshoppers." Askia outfitted his foot soldiers with armor and steel helmets.

He also built a navy that traveled up and down the mighty Niger River. Canals were dug to make it possible for merchants and farmers to move their goods more easily. From the north, caravans still traveled the trade routes across the Sahara, and the Songhay empire prospered.

Like Mansa Musa, Askia Muhammad made the *hajj* to Mecca and encouraged education throughout his realm by building schools and mosques. The most important center of learning was the University of Sankore in Timbuktu. It attracted students from throughout the Songhay empire. Scholars came to teach there from other parts of the Islamic world, beginning a scholarly tradition that lasted for many years.

Ahmed Baba was part of this proud tradition. His grandfather, al-Hajj Ahmad ("al-Hajj" means that he too had made the *hajj*, or pilgrimage to Mecca) lived during the reigns of Sunni Ali and Askia Muhammad. Al-Hajj Ahmad and his two brothers were widely known for their learning and devotion to Islam. Ahmed Baba later wrote that his grandfather "was a man of goodness, virtuous and pious...a very upright and distinguished man." He was proficient in many fields, including law, theology, science, and language. He traveled throughout the empire, teaching others. His prized possessions were books that he copied in his own hand, adding his own ideas and comments. He continued his work until he died at the age of eighty.

Ahmed Baba eagerly followed in his grandfather's footsteps. His brilliance brought him the honor of being named chancellor, or head, of the University of Sankore. Students flocked to hear his lectures on law, religion, and science.

He loved to relax with other scholars, discussing the newest books. In later years Ahmed Baba recalled that all his friends had more books than he did. Yet he owned 1,600 volumes, a large number for any private library of the time. He generously allowed others to borrow his books, following the example of one of his own beloved teachers. In turn he added to his library by copying out books that were new to him. An afternoon spent with his library was the most enjoyable pleasure in his life.

Ahmed Baba himself was the author of more than forty books. They included works on astronomy and commentaries on law and the Koran, the holy book of Islam. He started to assemble an encyclopedia of the teachings of Muslim religious leaders. But Ahmed Baba's peaceful life was disrupted by a great tragedy that shook the Songhay Empire.

After the death of Askia Muhammad the Great in 1528, Songhay's military power declined. The rich cities of the Songhay Empire attracted the greed of the Sultan of Morocco, on Africa's northern coast. The sultan invaded Songhay, sending an army south across the Sahara. Although the Moroccan forces were outnumbered by Songhay's, they had an important advantage—gunpowder and firearms. The spears of Songhay were no match for the guns of the Moroccan soldiers.

The invading troops caused widespread damage throughout West Africa. In 1591 the Moroccans captured several major cities of Songhay, including Timbuktu. The Moroccan soldiers plundered the homes of the city, stealing everything of value. Ahmed Baba helplessly watched as his beloved books were carried off. Moreover, the sultan coveted not only books but also scholars. His soldiers rounded up the teachers of the university and brought them in chains to Morocco.

Ahmed Baba was thrown into prison in Marrakesh, the Moroccan capital city, where he was held for over a year. He passed the time by giving lectures to the prison guards, who called him a "fount of wisdom." When he was released, he was led to the main mosque of Marrakesh. A crowd applauded him, for his name was well known.

Ahmed Baba loudly protested the sultan's unjust invasion of his country and demanded to see the ruler. Finally he was admitted to the palace of the sultan, Ahmad el-Mansour, who was curious about this unruly captive.

At their meeting Ahmed Baba demonstrated both his bravery and his skill at intellectual debate. When he was shown into the sultan's quarters, he found that the ruler was concealed behind a curtain. The sultan did not show himself to ordinary subjects.

Ahmed Baba said: "God has declared in the Koran that no human being can communicate with Him from behind a veil. If it is your wish to speak to me, come forth from behind that curtain." The startled sultan drew the curtain aside.

With great dignity, Ahmed Baba began to question the sultan. "What need had you to sack my house, steal my books, and put me into chains to bring me to Morocco? By means of those chains I fell from my camel and broke my leg."

The sultan replied that his purpose was to unite the Islamic nations. Ahmed Baba pointed out that the sultan had not chosen to attack his more powerful Islamic neighbors, the Turks. The sultan responded that Muhammad himself had advised his followers to leave the Turks in peace. Ahmed Baba searched his memory and came up with a quote from a later Islamic teacher who had contradicted this. The sultan realized that Ahmed Baba was too learned a man to argue with, and ordered him taken away.

Ahmed Baba was allowed his freedom within Marrakesh, but was not permitted to return home, for el-Mansour feared that he would stir up resistance against Moroccan rule. The scholars of

Marrakesh asked him to teach in their university, and the judges of Marrakesh's law courts regularly consulted him on difficult legal matters. His knowledge of Islamic law won him further respect. But Ahmed Baba was modest about his role, saying: "I carefully examined from every point of view the questions asked me, and having little confidence in my own judgment I entreated the assistance of God, and the Lord graciously enlightened me."

For twelve years Ahmed Baba was forced to remain in Marrakesh. During this time he wrote a book on the peoples of West Africa to enlighten the Moroccans about his native country. However, he could not even speak about his homeland without tears coming to his eyes. During his exile he wrote:

> O thou who goest to Gao, turn aside from thy path to breathe my name in Timbuktu. Bring there the greeting of an exile who sighs for the soil on which his friends and family reside. Console my near and dear ones for the deaths of those our lords, who have been entombed.

Finally, after the death of el-Mansour, a new sultan released Ahmed Baba. On the day he left, the important citizens of Marrakesh gathered to thank him for his services. At the moment of farewell, one man extended his hand and hailed the African with a verse from the Koran: "Certainly he who has made the Koran for thee shall lead you back here once more." This was a customary way of saying farewell and wishing a safe journey. But Ahmed Baba removed his hand and exclaimed, "May God never bring me back to this meeting, nor make me return to this country!"

Ahmed Baba grieved when he returned to Timbuktu for he found that many of his old friends were dead. He never regained his library. Worst of all, the Moroccan invasion had destroyed the peace and tranquility that enabled scholars like him to pursue their work. The University of Sankore never recovered from the arrest and captivity of its scholars. Ahmed Baba died in 1627.

Today, his descendants still live in the modern nation of Mali. An interesting tradition links them to their famous ancestor. When Ahmed Baba left Marrakesh, the new sultan presented him with a chair. Whenever one of Ahmed Baba's family is married, the groom is allowed to sit in the chair on the wedding day. By tradition he and his children will inherit the wisdom and goodness of the greatest scholar of Songhay.

C H A P T E R 5

BRASS THAT REMEMBERS— EUWARE THE GREAT

According to legend, the Bini—the people of ancient Benin—were unhappy with their leaders. So the Bini sent messengers to the holy city of Ife, far to the northwest. They asked Ife's *oni*, or ruler, to send one of his sons to rule Benin. Oduduwa, the oni of Ife, carefully considered the request. He did not want to risk one of his sons, for he did not know how reliable these Bini people were. Instead of a son, he sent seven lice for the Bini to take care of for three years. After the time passed, Oduduwa was pleased to see that the lice had increased in size. "The people," he declared, "who could take care of such minute pests could undoubtedly take care of my son."

So Prince Oranmiyan, one of Oduduwa's sons, came to Benin and married a beautiful young Bini woman. After a son was born to the couple, Prince Oranmiyan called the people together and gave up the throne. He told the Bini that their ruler should be a child born and raised in the arts and sciences of the country he would rule.

Oranmiyan's son thus became the first *oba*, or ruler, of Benin. He took the title Eweka, which means "I succeeded." Supposedly these were his first words as a baby. He spoke them after he had won a board game called akhue, with the aid of seven magic seeds given him by his father.

The obas who followed Eweka kept their close ties to Ife. That city had skilled artisans who made heads and statues from brass. When a later oba, named Oguola, saw the beautiful works of art, he wished that his own people could learn to make them too. Oguola asked the oni of Ife to send him a brass-smith.

Around the year 1200, a man named Iguegha answered the call. He went to Benin, where he delighted the Oba with his brass sculptures covered with ornate patterns and designs. He started the guild of brass-smiths, which still exists today. Because his talent was so powerful, the people of Benin worshiped Iguegha as a god after his death.

The brass art works of Benin are famous throughout the world for their extraordinary beauty. They were used in religious and political ceremonies, but also had another purpose. The brass-smiths depicted scenes from the life of each oba of Benin, and thus provided a way to remember and record the history of the country.

Ife and Benin were two of the forest kingdoms that arose in what is today Nigeria, south of the empires of Ghana, Mali, and Songhay. Their people produced magnificent sculptures in brass, stone, and *terra cotta*, or baked clay. Sub-Saharan Africa abounds in art of all kinds, but the people of this area were the only ones to make human figures that were almost life-sized.

The tradition is very old. Starting as early as the fifth century B.C., the people of a culture called Nok fashioned terra cotta figures of people and animals. The human faces were highly stylized, although the animals were done in lifelike fashion. Even today in some parts of Africa, sculptors do not strive to produce natural-looking human faces, for fear of being accused of witchcraft. This may be the reason why the Nok people used different artistic styles to represent people and animals.

At the city of Ife, the high artistic tradition continued. But Ife's artists and craftspeople created naturalistic, lifelike human figures and faces. In addition, they adopted new materials for their artistic masterpieces. One of these materials was brass, a combination of copper and zinc that has a shiny, gold-like appearance and a harder surface than copper alone.

In the full-length figures the heads were made larger than they would be in real life. For the people of Ife believed that the head was the center of the soul. Ancestor worship was an important part of religion and these heads kept alive the memories of the dead who watch over the living. The spirit world and the everyday world were thus united.

Heads of the oni were sculpted to use in various rituals and ceremonies and placed in shrines within the palace. Some of the faces were cast with vertical lines running down their lengths. These lines are believed to represent strings of beads that the oni wore on his head, hanging down right over his face.

The Ife and Benin brasses are very unusual. They were made only in this relatively small part of Africa. People in other places had not discovered the secret of casting brass into such perfect sculptures. The process is called the "lost-wax" method, in which a sculptor begins by making a clay model. The sculptor covers the model with a thin coating of wax, and then another coating of clay. Holes are left in the bottom so that when the clay is baked, the wax melts and runs out. Then molten brass is poured inside. After the brass cools, the outer clay covering is broken away, revealing a brass sculpture.

This was the secret knowledge that the brass-smith Iguegha brought to Benin. In the early years the Bini copied Ife but soon developed their own styles. They began to make three-dimensional plaques for the doors and walls of the palace. These plaques were more than merely decoration. They were the equivalent of history books.

Benin, like Ife, had no written form of its language. Its traditions, religion, and history were carried on from generation to generation through oral tradition. Court remembrancers were trained by their elders to memorize the stories and facts that were important.

The brass plaques made this task easier. By looking at them, a remembrancer could describe the events they showed—for example, weddings of the obas and royal hunting parties. The proper ceremonial forms, individual rulers, their families, and officials were all portrayed on the plaques, and the remembrancers memorized their names.

In the early 1400s trouble came to Benin. The oba became displeased with his two sons and sent them into exile. After the oba died, the elder son sent his brother back to see if the Bini wanted him as their leader. But the younger brother lied, claiming that he had not seen his brother since they left the city. As a result, he persuaded the people to name him oba.

When his older brother, whose name was Ogun, learned this, he was filled with anger. Ogun armed himself and made war against his brother. The fighting was fierce, for both brothers had many followers. A great part of the capital city was destroyed. Ogun finally won when he surprised his brother in the market place and killed him. Ogun became oba and gave himself the title

Euware, which literally means "It is cool." The word was understood as "The trouble is over."

Euware was a very able ruler, and his people remembered him as Euware Ogidigan, which means "Euware the Great." His first achievement was to rebuild his capital city, which he named Edo (today's Benin City, in Nigeria). Running through the entire city was a broad avenue that a later visitor, from Holland, described as being many times wider than the main street of Amsterdam. Of the houses along the streets, this visitor said they "stand in good order, one close and even beside the other as the houses in Holland stand."

Euware was a mighty warrior. The plaques show him fighting in his full war regalia. Bini warriors carried spears, bows and arrows, and shields of bamboo or woven reeds. It is said that Euware conquered 210 villages during his term as oba.

Such a powerful ruler was entitled to take many wives. Indeed, hundreds of them lived in Euware's palace, but he was always looking for more. He heard about the three beautiful daughters of a chief who lived in his domains. Euware asked the chief to send his eldest daughter, named Ubi, to the palace. The chief warned Euware that Ubi was a poor choice for a wife, because she refused to respect any man.

Euware insisted, and Ubi was sent to him. She was worse than her father had warned. She would not even speak to the oba and was unfriendly to the other women in the household. She made everyone unhappy. Oba Euware carried a pouch full of magic charms, and thought that he could use them to entice Ubi. But nothing worked, and finally Euware sent her away. As she left, the women of the palace beat her with burning sticks, calling *Ubi rie, Ubi rie*, which means, "Ubi, go."

Euware was hard to discourage. He asked for the chief's second daughter, named Ewere. She proved to be a sweet-tempered woman, and everyone became fond of her. The other women of the palace danced at her arrival. Yet Ewere sometimes wept when she thought no one could hear her. When her husband discovered this, she told him she missed her younger sister, Oyoyo, and asked the oba to bring her to the palace. The oba agreed, and when Oyoyo arrived, he decided to marry her as well.

Euware was so happy with his new wives that he celebrated

the anniversary of the marriage to Ewere at the Igue festival. He sacrificed goats, cows, and leopards to the gods and also made offerings of kola nuts and coconuts for good luck. Whirling acrobats spun from ropes attached to trees. Yam cakes, pots of palm oils, and bunches of plantains were offered to the guests. The Igue festival is still celebrated today in Benin City.

People of the region still try to avoid making a journey on "Ubi day," when Ubi left the palace. They postpone their trips until "Ewere day," the anniversary of Ewere's arrival.

In 1472, the year before Euware's death, the first Europeans visited Benin. The palace plaques show them with such accuracy that modern historians can identify them as Portuguese. Later, Dutch and British arrived as well. All were dazzled by the work of Benin's brass-smiths. Their art became important in the trade between Europeans and Africans. The Bini artisans began to make items specifically for the European market, such as finely wrought salt-cellars and religious objects. This was one of the first examples of artists creating works especially for visitors.

In the twentieth century, Jacob Egharevba, a descendant of one of Oba Euware's officers, used the oral traditions and the brass plaques to write a history of Benin. Much of the information we have used in this chapter comes from Egharevba's book. It is the story of a people who produced some of the most brilliant artists in history.

CHAPTER 6

THE WARRIOR QUEEN—
ANN NZINGA

In the year 1622 a woman named Nzinga arrived at the trading post of Luanda (the capital of today's Angola). Luanda was the headquarters of the Portuguese viceroy in western Africa. Nzinga's brother, the *ngola*, or king, of Ndongo, had sent her to arrange a peace treaty between his people and the Portuguese.

The Portuguese had built a large hut in front of the viceroy's residence for Nzinga and her escorts. She traveled with a large group of attendants, many of them women. All were treated with respect and honor by the Portuguese, and Nzinga was pleased.

However, when she was ushered inside the viceroy's official meeting room, her eyes darkened in anger. A glance around the room showed only one seat of honor—the viceroy's magnificent chair. On the floor was a gold embroidered cushion for Nzinga to sit on. That was not acceptable to her. The ambassador of the ngola of Ndongo should not sit at anyone's feet.

Nzinga nodded at one of her female attendants. Without a word, the young woman stepped forward and knelt on her hands and knees. Coolly, Nzinga sat down on her attendant's back.

Now that both parties were on the same level, the negotiations began. The viceroy pointed out what both knew—his soldiers had been fighting Ndongo's for some time, and neither side had been able to defeat the other. It was time, the viceroy suggested, for Portugal and Ndongo to become allies. Ndongo would benefit, for by trading with Portugal it could obtain many desirable goods. The fighting would stop. But the viceroy asked that Ndongo pay an annual tribute to the King of Portugal.

Nzinga briskly refused the offer. She would ask her brother to stop the fighting if the Portuguese wished to end the war, but a ngola did not pay tribute. The only concession she was willing to

make was to turn over the Portuguese prisoners that Ndongo had captured. Finally the viceroy accepted her terms, impressed by her spirit and regal bearing.

When the negotiations ended, the viceroy saw Nzinga to the door. Her attendants followed, except for the woman who still knelt on the floor. The viceroy asked why Nzinga had not told her to rise. Nzinga answered haughtily: "It is not fitting that the ambassador of a great king should be served with the same seat twice. I have no further use for the woman." The viceroy was astonished, but Nzinga was a woman whose actions often amazed those who opposed her.

Nzinga was born about 1583 in the northern part of today's Angola, in southwest Africa. Her family was part of the group called the Jagas, known both to their neighbors and later to the Portuguese as fierce warriors. The Jagas had developed the skill of forging iron, which they used for weapons. Indeed, their ngola (the word from which the name of the modern country comes) was known not only as king, but also as the chief blacksmith. With their iron weapons, the Jagas conquered some of their neighbors to form the kingdom of Ndongo. Other kingdoms, such as the Kongo, also existed in this part of Africa when Portuguese ships appeared on the coast in the late fifteenth century.

The Portuguese were seeking a sea route to the East Indies— the islands that were the sources of precious spices that brought high prices in Europe. As the Portuguese gradually made their way down the west coast of Africa, they established trading posts where future voyages could take on supplies. Luanda, one of these posts, had been founded in 1576.

The African trade, however, soon became important to Portugal. Along the coast far north of Ndongo, the Portuguese obtained such things as ivory, gold, and the beautiful sculptures of Benin's craftspeople. The Portuguese sometimes paid for these with cloth and jewelry. But the product that Africans most desired was the musket, an early type of rifle that was far more powerful than the spears and arrows the Africans had.

The people of southwest Africa, where Nzinga lived, wanted muskets too, but had no gold or ivory to trade for them. The Portuguese demanded slaves as trade goods. By this time Portugal controlled a huge colony in America, Brazil. To work the plantations and mines there, the Portuguese needed African slaves.

Africans had kept slaves before the Portuguese arrived. Usually the slaves were captives taken in battle. But they were well treated, and might even return to their homelands when warring groups made peace and traded prisoners. Slaves could also buy their freedom by selling produce that they grew on their own plots of land.

Slaves taken by the Portuguese, however, were treated quite differently. They were packed into ships as tightly as a load of lumber, and were never seen again after the ships disappeared over the horizon. No one knows the exact number, but it is estimated that at least a million people from Angola alone were uprooted from their homeland and taken to America.

Later, cotton plantations in North America also used slaves from Angola. On certain islands off the coast of South Carolina today live African-Americans called Gullahs. The Gullahs in these isolated places have preserved many of the customs and music, as well as the language of their Angolan ancestors.

All those who survived the harrowing voyage across the Atlantic were put in chains and literally worked to death. The loss of so many of its people—and millions more taken by other European nations—kept Africa from developing the industry, science, and agriculture that would have enabled its people to prosper. The four centuries from the arrival of the Europeans to the mid-twentieth century brought misery and suffering to virtually every sub-Saharan African nation.

The Portuguese traders stayed in their bases on the coast. They employed Africans to capture or purchase slaves farther inland. When necessary, the Portuguese trained Africans as soldiers, arming them with muskets, to conquer and enslave other Africans. Nzinga's country, Ndongo, was among those who lost young men and women to the "slave soldiers" of the Portuguese.

Nzinga's brother was Ngoli Bbondi, the reigning ngola of Ndongo. As a young girl, Nzinga burned with the desire to stop the Portuguese slave-traders from raiding the kingdom. Her brother fought them so successfully that the Portuguese viceroy finally offered to negotiate.

Nzinga's excursion to Luanda was the first major achievement of her career. After her meeting with the viceroy, she stayed for a while in the European outpost. She met some of the Catholic priests who accompanied the Portuguese soldiers, and she is said to have converted to Christianity at this time. She may have been truly inspired by the religion, or may only have felt the gesture to be helpful in dealing with the Portuguese. After her baptism she took the name Ann.

Soon after Nzinga returned to her kingdom, her brother, the ngola, died. Ambitious for power, Nzinga acted with ruthless decisiveness. She strangled her nephew so that she could take the throne. She refused to be called the queen, instead taking the title *ngola*, formerly reserved only for men. She dressed in men's clothes when she led her warriors into battle. Nzinga built up her army, for she did not trust the Portuguese. Her personal guard was composed of women who trained with bows and arrows.

The Portuguese viceroy, hearing of Nzinga's preparations for war, decided to get rid of her. He ordered his soldiers to attack her

territory. Despite the bravery of Nzinga and her warriors, the Africans were not able to overcome the modern weaponry of the Portuguese. Nzinga once more tried to negotiate a peace treaty. The Portuguese offered to allow her to retain her throne if she would agree to pay the annual tribute. The proud ngola refused and fled into the interior of the country with her troops. She conquered the kingdom of Matamba and continued to fight from there.

The war was a long one. For twenty years, Nzinga's forces successfully defended their land against the Portuguese. In her desperate situation she needed all her talents to survive. Nzinga had a strong personality that could charm one moment and inspire fear the next. She renounced Christianity and called on other Africans to join her in driving out the Portuguese. She made a special appeal to the African "slave soldiers," appealing to their sense of pride in their African heritage. Nzinga offered them freedom and land if they would desert the Portuguese and join her cause. Many did.

She tried to bring other African kings over to her side with the same message. Nzinga thought that if the Africans united under one ruler, they would be able to defeat the Portuguese. She intended to be that ruler. She could be ruthless to anyone who opposed her, and made war on African states who refused her offers of alliance. Nzinga was as skillful a diplomat as she was a warrior. She looked around for another European ally. The Dutch had also set up trading posts in Africa, and Nzinga asked them to help her fight the Portuguese. The Dutch were only too willing to oblige, and sent some of their troops to Nzinga's territory.

A Dutch officer commanding the troops was impressed by the female African ruler. He described Nzinga as "a cunning and prudent virago [fierce woman], so much addicted to arms that she hardly uses other exercise." But he also noted that she was so honorable that "she never hurt a Portuguese after quarter was given and commanded all her servants and soldiers alike."

Nzinga was shaken by a tragic event that occurred in 1645. Her sister Fungi was captured by the Portuguese. They beheaded her and tossed her body into a river. Nzinga grieved for her sister. The loss made her wonder whether the Christian religion was not in fact stronger than her own beliefs. Her own god, Tem-Bon-Dumba, had not protected Fungi. He had not been as strong as the Christian god.

Yet Nzinga had also heard from missionaries that the Christian god was a just one, who wanted to end the suffering of all people. If this was so, why did the Portuguese take her people as slaves? Why did they invade the lands of others and burn their houses?

She could not answer these questions, but as time went on she saw that it was useless to resist. Many of her most faithful warriors had died in battle, yet the Portuguese still sent their soldiers against her. Nzinga again decided to accept the Christian religion, and in 1659, when she was seventy-five, finally came to terms with the Portuguese. They too were tired of the fighting and this time did not demand that she pay tribute.

She continued to rule the kingdom of Matamba to the end of her life. She built a church for the Portuguese missionaries, and she ordered her subjects to convert to Christianity. Nzinga announced that polygamy and human sacrifice to the old gods were forbidden. These commands made her unpopular, but to set an example she herself, who had never taken a husband, married one of her courtiers when she was seventy-six.

In her last years, Nzinga became more devoted to Christianity. She sent a message to the pope asking that he send more missionaries to her kingdom. When the pope's reply arrived, she had it read aloud at a great ceremony in the church she had built. In honor of the occasion, Nzinga and her female guards dressed as they had for war and staged a mock battle. Spectators noted that despite her age, the old ngola fought with as much energy as the younger warriors.

In 1663 Ann Nzinga died at the age of eighty-one. Her subjects gathered to mourn the ruler who had led them for so long. Fittingly, her body was displayed in royal robes, with a bow and arrow in her hands. But at her own request, that was not the way she was buried. The priests dressed her in the habit of a Catholic monk and replaced the bow and arrow with a crucifix and rosary. In the end, Ann Nzinga had decided to make her peace with the Christian god.

After her death the kingdom fell into the hands of the Portuguese. Angola would not regain its independence until 1974. Ann Nzinga, however, lived on in the legends of the people of Angola. Her life story is the subject of a book by one of modern Angola's best writers.

C H A P T E R 7

"GIVE US FREE"—CINQUE

It was midnight on board the slave ship *Amistad*. The only sounds were the slapping of water against the hull and the creaking of the masts as the wind filled the sails. The helmsman who steered the ship expected no trouble, for the fifty-four slaves aboard were securely chained to each other. Since this was expected to be a short voyage, the slaves were allowed to sleep on deck. A few days earlier, they had been sold to the highest bidders in a Cuban market and were now being transported to the Caribbean island of Haiti. Two of their owners were also on board and wanted their valuable "cargo" to arrive in good health.

But one of the slaves, a man named Cinque, was awake. Earlier in the day, he had pried a loose nail from one of the deck boards. Now he slipped the nail into the lock that secured his chains. Patiently, he worked the nail back and forth. When it scraped against the iron lock, he stopped to see if the noise had alerted the helmsman.

At last, the lock popped open. Cinque poked awake the four men who were sleeping next to him. Now that he had learned how to pick the locks, he swiftly freed them as well. The five Africans crept across the deck and slipped into the hold. Cinque's sharp eyes had seen a crew member stow away a crate of cutlasses. Somehow, in the darkness, the Africans pried open the crate and armed themselves.

Back on deck, they moved stealthily toward the helmsman. At the last moment, he saw them and cried out. In seconds, the captain and crew were on deck, fighting for their lives. Men from both sides fell bleeding to the deck. The captain killed two of the Africans before Cinque sliced off his head with a single blow.

Seeing the captain fall, the crew ran for the lifeboats. They were seamen, not soldiers, and they had not signed on to risk their lives against a mob of ferocious slaves.

"Let them go!" Cinque called out to his men. He swiftly freed the rest of the Africans. Cinque had a plan—a wild, daring scheme that seemed almost impossible. The strange voyage of the *Amistad* would make Cinque one of the most famous of the millions of Africans who were forced from their homeland into slavery.

Cinque was born about 1811 in the village of Mani, in the country of the Mendi people of West Africa (today's Sierra Leone). His father was the headman of the village, and Cinque was raised as a warrior prince. The Mendi were always on guard against their neighbors, for the European slave traders encouraged wars among the different peoples of Africa. The Europeans bought captives from both sides. Former enemies found themselves chained together on the slave ships that left Africa for the Americas.

When Cinque was about twenty-eight, he was ambushed and captured not far from his village. He soon was imprisoned in the *barracoon*, or slave warehouse, of Don Pedro Blanco, a notorious slave trader on the coast. Before long, Cinque was taken aboard a ship and forced into the hold. He began the terrible "middle passage" that brought some thirty million Africans to the New World during the three centuries that the slave trade was carried on.

No one knows how many people died on these ghastly voyages—a typical slave ship lost about one-third of its human cargo in the fifty-day journey. The Africans were chained side-by-side with only enough room to lie down. The ceiling of the hold was too low for anyone to stand, and people gasped for a breath of air. A doctor on one of the ships said that the heat and stench in the hold were so bad that he could stand it only for a few minutes. What must it have been like to endure it for nearly two months?

When disease swept through the "black cargo," the crew pulled up the dead bodies each morning to throw them over the side. Sharks commonly followed the slave ships across the Atlantic, waiting for the meals that were regularly served. On the rare occasions when slaves were allowed on deck, many jumped over the side, choosing to drown rather than go back to the horrors below.

Cinque was strong. He survived, and when the ship reached Havana, Cuba, he suddenly found himself well treated. Kept in another barracoon, the Africans were given decent food and water for the first time since they left Africa. Cinque realized that they were being fattened up, like cattle for market.

Cinque held himself proudly at the slave auction. He refused to open his mouth to let his teeth be examined. Yet his strong body attracted a buyer—Don José Ruiz, who owned a sugar plantation in Haiti. Don José felt that the overseer's whip would tame the spirit of this haughty African, and then he would become a good worker.

Don José brought his new slaves on board the ship *Amistad*, and shared the cost of the voyage with his friend Don Pedro Montez, who had a few slaves of his own to transport. Don José brought along an older slave, who had been his personal servant for many years.

When they heard the uproar on deck, the two Spaniards locked the doors of their cabin. They remained there until morning, not knowing what had happened. Then they heard a voice outside the door, speaking in a strange African language. Don José's servant recognized it—as luck would have it, he came from the same part of Africa as Cinque.

Using him to translate, Cinque offered a bargain. He would spare the Spaniards' lives. In return, they would steer the ship for him. Cinque wanted only one thing—to return to Africa. After the Spaniards had brought the Africans home, they could find a crew and return to Cuba.

The Spaniards agreed, but they did not intend to let their valuable slaves escape so easily. They too had a scheme. During the day, when Cinque could see by the sun which direction they were sailing, the Spaniards dutifully guided the ship eastward toward Africa.

At night, however, the Spaniards secretly turned the ship in the other direction. They could also veer off course on cloudy or rainy days. But neither Spaniard was an expert navigator, and they failed to return to Cuba, as they had planned.

For six weeks, the *Amistad* zigzagged back and forth in the Atlantic Ocean. The food and water on board soon ran out, but fortunately the voyagers sighted an uninhabited island where they took on water, and they pulled enough fish from the ocean to survive.

No one on board knew that the ship was now the object of an international search. The sailors who had gone over the side had made their way back to Cuba and raised an alarm. Ships from Spain, Britain, and the United States were on the lookout for the *Amistad*. Once, a fishing boat sighted the wayward ship, but when its crew saw Africans on deck with cutlasses, they kept their distance. Newspapers in the United States printed the story.

Finally, the African lookout on the *Amistad*'s masthead shouted that he could see land. Everyone rushed to the side of the ship, straining their eyes for a sight of their homeland. Instead, they saw white wooden houses that looked nothing like those of Africa.

Even so, Cinque let down the anchor, for the supplies had run out again. Cinque had found golden coins in the cabins below and knew that he could use them to buy food. Taking some of his men in a small boat, he went ashore.

The *Amistad* had come a long way. It had reached Montauk Point on the eastern tip of Long Island, New York. The townspeople were astonished when a group of nearly naked Africans marched into their town with fistfuls of Spanish doubloons.

But the voyage ended there. While Cinque was ashore, a United States warship, the *Washington*, sighted the *Amistad* at anchor. The *Washington*'s captain sent a boarding party armed with muskets, and the Africans surrendered. Cinque and the others on shore were soon captured as well.

Don José Ruiz produced papers that showed he owned the Africans and demanded that they be turned over to him at once. But the captain of the *Washington* put in his own claim for salvaging the ship and its cargo. The *Amistad* was towed across Long Island Sound to New Haven, Connecticut, where a judge would sort out the matter.

Don José Ruiz was worried, for he didn't want anyone to look too closely at his claim to the Africans. Slavery was still legal in the Spanish colonies (including Cuba) and in the United States. However, both Spain and the United States had outlawed the practice of importing new slaves from Africa. The deed of sale for the Africans said that they were *Ladinos*—slaves born in the New World who could still be bought and sold. The Africans could testify that this was a lie, but since no one in the area could speak their language except his own servant, Don José hoped that the judge would not discover the truth. Just to make sure, he sent a message to the Spanish ambassador in Washington, D.C., asking him to intercede with the United States government.

However, Cinque soon acquired important friends. Many people in the northern United States were abolitionists, who advocated ending slavery altogether. Newspapers began to print sympathetic stories about the *"Amistad* mutiny." Lewis Tappan, a wealthy merchant in New York City, saw a drawing of Cinque in a newspaper and was touched by this young African's struggle to free himself and his companions. Tappan hired a lawyer to represent the Africans, and also found a free African sailor who could speak the Mandean language.

The president of the United States at this time was Martin Van Buren, who had won election with Southern slaveholders' support. His secretary of state, a slaveowner himself, wrote a letter to the United States district attorney in New Haven, warning him not to allow the court to free the Africans.

When the letter became public, it outraged many Americans. Abolitionist groups began to contribute funds to help Cinque win his freedom in court. Meanwhile, he and the other Africans were kept in the New Haven jail all through the winter of 1839-40. They had never experienced cold weather like this before, and when some died, the townspeople donated blankets for them.

Finally, in January 1840, the case came before Judge A.T. Judson. In earlier cases Judge Judson had ordered escaped slaves returned to their owners. But at the climax of the trial, Cinque rose and asked to speak. Through a translator, he related everything that had happened since he had been captured near his village.

The spectators listened in horrified fascination as the tall black man, a blanket draped over his shoulders, related his experiences in the hell of a slave ship's hold in the Atlantic. He told of seeing an African whipped mercilessly for trying to steal a cup of water. He described men, women, and children suffering and dying next to each other day after day, forced to lie in their own wastes. Few other Africans had ever given eyewitness testimony to the horrors of the "middle passage." But no one could doubt that Cinque spoke the truth. Finally, Cinque looked at the judge and spoke three of the English words he had learned that winter: "Give...us...free!"

Judge Judson was touched by the plea. He ordered that the Africans should be turned over to the President of the United States and as soon as possible returned to Africa. The courtroom broke into cheers.

President Van Buren, however, would not accept the decision. He faced a re-election campaign later that year and needed

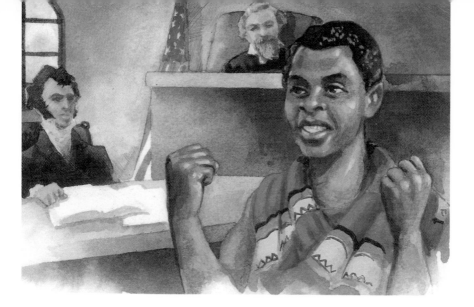

Southern support. He ordered that the case be appealed to a higher court. It dragged on for another year and in February 1841 reached the Supreme Court.

A new lawyer volunteered to plead the Africans' case. He was John Quincy Adams, a former president of the United States and son of one of the nation's founders. Though he was now seventy-three, Adams spoke before the court for eight and a half hours, calling the Africans "fellow men...seized, imprisoned, helpless, friendless, without language to complain." He appealed to the Court to save them "from slavery and death."

The justices agreed, and at last Cinque and his friends were free. By now Cinque was so famous that abolitionist groups asked him to appear before anti-slavery meetings throughout the United States. It was another year before he finally returned home. Five missionaries, two of them ex-slaves, accompanied him.

Sadly, Cinque found that his wife and children had disappeared, probably to slavers, during his own captivity. He started a new family, living on to the age of sixty-eight. Before he died, he asked to be baptized a Christian, for he remembered fondly the Americans who saw him as a man like themselves. The name on his grave is Joseph Cinque.

He stands for the unknown millions of Africans who made the middle passage to slavery. Though no history book contains their names, they too lived and died with memories of their homeland calling them back to freedom.

C H A P T E R   8

"The Beginning of a New Day"—
Menelik II and Taitu

During Easter week of 1883, a man and woman stood before the altar of a Christian church in the city of Ankober, Ethiopia. The fragrance of incense and the chanting of priests filled the dark recesses of the sanctuary. In front of their distinguished guests, the couple was married by the *abuna*, or bishop.

The groom, Menelik, was the *ras*, or king, of Shoa, a territory in southern Ethiopia. According to one who knew him, he was

> stoutly built and about six feet in height. His skin was very dark....He had a good broad forehead and very bright, intelligent eyes....He wore a mustache and a short, curly beard. His expression was good, and when lighted up by a pleasant smile, his face was very attractive....His manners were dignified and kindly, and his gracious courtesy endeared him to all people; his speech was simple and direct.

The bride, Taitu, was a princess from the northern kingdom of Tigre. She was slim and lovely in her *shammas*, a long gown with embroidery along the edges. Her hair was braided across her head in tight rows. She wore gold necklaces and, in the northern style, tied silver bells and beads around her ankles.

The marriage of Menelik and Taitu united two people who were devoted to Ethiopia. They shepherded their country through times of crisis and danger. Because of them, Ethiopia survived foreign threats and became one of the only two African nations to remain independent from European colonial rule.

Sahle Mariam (Menelik's birth name) was born in 1844 in the town of Ankober about 100 miles northeast of today's Addis Ababa. He was the son of Ras Haile Malakot of Shoa. Sahle took great pride in his family, which was able to trace its ancestors all the

way back to King Solomon and the Queen of Sheba.

However, he grew up in dangerous times. For the last hundred years, the *negus nagast* (king of kings) of Ethiopia had been little more than a figurehead. The greatest unifying force in the country was the Ethiopian Christian Church. Real power rested with local rulers like Sahle's father. Bandits roamed the land raiding and robbing traders. The breakdown of law and order enabled one of these bandits to seize the throne in 1855. As emperor, he took the name Tewodros, or Theodore. He was determined to control the country and sent his army to conquer the independent kingdoms. Theodore defeated Shoa and took the eleven-year-old Prince Sahle and his mother as hostages.

For ten years Sahle lived in the fortress of Amba Mekdala. He was well treated, receiving an education from tutors. At Theodore's court, he met Europeans that the emperor had invited to help modernize his country.

Yet Sahle dreamed of restoring his father's kingdom. Theodore faced continual rebellions within his empire, and in 1865 Sahle seized a chance to escape. During the summer, he fled with his mother and a few other hostages. Sahle issued a bold call to Theodore's opponents all over the country: "I have arrived. Send men to receive me." He returned to Shoa, where the people acclaimed him as their rightful king. To stress the link with his famous ancestors, Sahle took the name Menelik II. (Menelik I was the legendary son of King Solomon and the Queen of Sheba.)

Meanwhile, Theodore made a crucial mistake. He imprisoned some British officials after a trade dispute. Britain sent troops to Ethiopia to free them. Many Ethiopians saw this as a chance to overthrow Theodore and welcomed the British. The emperor committed suicide in 1868.

Fighting broke out among the kings who hoped to become the new emperor. Menelik was among them, but eventually he made an alliance with the ras of Tigre, an area in the northern part of the country. The ras of Tigre became emperor under the name Yohannes, promising that Menelik would be his successor and giving him a free hand in ruling Shoa. Yohannes cemented their alliance by offering Menelik the hand of Taitu in marriage.

Secretly, Yohannes hoped that Taitu would serve as his spy in Menelik's court. Instead, however, she became one of her husband's closest and most loyal advisers. Confident and ambitious, she helped him steer a careful course in making alliances with Europeans and Africans alike. Taitu's shrewd, calculating mind often balanced Menelik's hot tempered, impulsive nature.

On a high, windy plain in a southern part of his territory, Menelik established a military outpost. Nearby, Taita found a sunny, wooded valley where hot springs flowed. Bathing in the springs helped her rheumatism, so she built a *katama*, or residence, there. Taitu named the valley Addis Ababa, or "New Flower." A town grew up around Taitu's katama, and when Menelik became emperor, he made Addis Ababa his capital.

Yohannes' fourteen-year reign ended when he was killed while fighting Muslim invaders from the Sudan. By that time, Menelik was the most powerful man in the kingdom, and there was no doubt that he should be the new emperor.

On November 3, 1889, princes and priests dressed in glittering robes assembled in the Church of Mary on Mount Entotto. The patriarch of the Ethiopian Christian Church crowned Menelik II *negus negast*, emperor of the Ethiopians. Two days later, in a similarly grand ceremony, Taitu received the title of empress. Because warfare had caused famine in much of the country, Menelik and Taitu ordered that the *gebers*, or feasts of celebration, be modest ones.

The new emperor and empress faced serious threats from foreign aggressors. The Europeans were no longer satisfied with trading posts in Africa. With their superior weaponry, the European nations were carving up the continent among themselves. Britain had already established domination over Egypt, and its soldiers had moved into the Sudan as well.

Menelik saw that the fighting between African nations weakened them and opened the way for European domination. He wrote to the ruler of Islamic Sudan, long an enemy of Ethiopia, and advised him, "Do not let the Europeans enter between us. Be strong, lest if the Europeans enter our midst a great disaster befall us and our children have no rest."

The most serious threat to Ethiopia came from the newly united nation of Italy, whose army had conquered Eritrea, a strip of Ethiopian territory along the Red Sea. Menelik decided to use diplomacy to deal with the Italians. In 1889 he signed an agreement in which he gave up Eritrea in return for Italian recognition of his status as emperor. In addition, Italy agreed to allow Ethiopia an outlet to the sea through its territory. This would enable Menelik to continue to buy modern arms to strengthen his army.

However, a dispute soon arose over a clause in the treaty. Two versions had been written—one in Italian, one in Amharic, the Ethiopian language. The Italian ambassador informed Menelik that the treaty barred Ethiopia from making agreements with other nations without first consulting Italy. Menelik claimed that the treaty gave him the *choice* of seeking Italy's advice, but only if he wished to.

Menelik wrote a letter to Italy's King Umberto, saying that "no independent power could ever make such a concession." The ambassador delivered the reply. King Umberto could not agree with Menelik's interpretation of the treaty, because "It would wound the dignity and pride of the Italian people."

Menelik stoutly responded, "If you have your dignity, we have ours too." Empress Taitu added, "I am a woman and I do not love war; but rather than accepting this I prefer war."

In 1893 Menelik canceled the treaty and Italian troops moved into Ethiopia's territory. Italy offered support to Menelik's rivals if they would rise against him. Menelik realized that unless he had the support of a united country, he could not win. He sent out a call to all Ethiopian leaders—friends and enemies alike—to meet him at the town of Boromeda. In stirring language he appealed to them to save the country. "We cannot," he said,

> permit our integrity as a Christian civilized nation to be questioned, nor the right to govern our empire in absolute independence....Ethiopia has never been conquered and she shall never be. We shall call no one to our defense. We are capable of protecting ourselves. Ethiopia will stretch forth her hands only to God!

His words brought an enthusiastic response. From all parts of Ethiopia, soldiers came to save their nation's independence. Menelik assembled his forces at Adowa, a town in the Tigre region near the ancient holy city of Axum.

On the night of February 29, 1896, the Italian troops marched toward Adowa. Knowing that the following day was an Ethiopian religious holiday, the Italians believed Menelik's soldiers would be celebrating in Axum. Thus, although the Italians were outnumbered, they could stage a surprise attack and destroy the army piecemeal.

However, Menelik's scouts had spotted the Italians. He sent soldiers into the mountains that surrounded the valley where the battle would take place. The rest of his army waited on the plain below, blocking the Italian advance. Early on the morning of March 1, the Italian commander ordered his artillery to open fire on Menelik's army. The Ethiopians suffered heavy losses from the bombardment. But when the Italian soldiers moved forward, they were caught in Menelik's trap. His soldiers in the mountains swarmed down from the heights, attacking the Italians from all sides.

The battle soon became a rout. The Italians tried to retreat, but had no place to go. Mercilessly, Menelik's men slaughtered them by the thousands. All their supplies and cannons fell into Menelik's hands. An Ethiopian painter later depicted the scene, showing both Menelik and Empress Taitu on the battlefield, with a servant holding a parasol over the empress's head.

Adowa was the greatest victory an African nation had won over Europeans in 2,000 years. The news caused a sensation throughout the world. "The white man is no longer considered a superior being," wrote a Frenchman at the time. "[Adowa] is an event which is for Africa, the beginning of a new day."

Disgraced, the Italian government was forced to resign. The smoldering humiliation would last into the twentieth century. In 1935 Italian dictator Benito Mussolini sought revenge against Menelik's great-nephew Haile Selassie, by invading Ethiopia again. By using poison gas, Italy triumphed, and held the nation for seven years.

But that was far in the future. Menelik now turned to the task of modernizing his country. The emperor worked tirelessly to build an Ethiopia whose trade, agriculture, and industry would be the equal of any nation's. In the mornings he received foreign diplomats trying to win his favor. Then came the officials he had put in charge of new building projects. All day long people came to him— doctors who discussed health regulations, traders showing their wares, arms dealers, tax collectors. Menelik personally carried on all the business of a large empire. He found time to discuss the nation's affairs with his beloved empress, who brought to his attention matters that he might have overlooked.

Any of their subjects could bring personal problems or complaints to Menelik and Taitu, who gave them a sympathetic hearing. Menelik had great pity and compassion for the least fortunate. During a famine, he set an example by tilling the fields like a farmer. When a cattle disease destroyed the herds so that only the wealthy could afford meat, Menelik refused to allow meat to be served in the palace. Instead he shared the royal herds with starving Ethiopians. On Christian holy days, Taitu served feasts in a huge hall in the palace to anyone who showed up at the door.

Yet Menelik always demanded absolute respect from Europeans. When a French prince appeared at his court dressed in hunting clothes, Menelik was indignant. "Who is this person," he declared, "who does not know how to appear before a king?"

Menelik died in 1913, after a long illness. Taitu retired to her beloved katama, where she lived for another five years. Ethiopia mourned at their deaths. These two people united and built an African nation that successfully resisted European conquest. Only Ethiopia and Liberia, a west-coast nation founded by freed slaves from the United States, kept their independence during the sad centuries when Africa was carved up into European colonies. Today, Taitu's favorite home, where she and Menelik spent many happy hours, is the capital city of a modern nation.

C H A P T E R 9

"SELF-GOVERNMENT NOW"—
KWAME NKRUMAH

A gentle breeze blew over New York harbor on a beautiful day in May 1945. The passengers on a departing ship had a good view of the Statue of Liberty that stands in the harbor as a beacon of freedom. To thirty-six-year old Kwame Nkrumah, a visitor from the British colony of the Gold Coast, it was a special moment. For the past ten years he had lived in the United States. Often he had been lonely and poor, yet he believed he had learned much. As he gazed at the Statue of Liberty, her torch appeared to be raised in a personal farewell just for him. He made a promise to her at that moment. "You have opened my eyes to the true meaning of liberty. I shall never rest until I have carried your message to Africa."

Kwame Nkrumah would keep that vow. Less than twelve years later, he led the Gold Coast to independence. His new nation, Ghana, was the first African state south of the Sahara to win freedom from European colonial rule.

Francis Nwia Kwame Nkrumah was born in 1909 in the little village of Nkroful, a few miles from the west coast of today's Ghana. His parents belonged to the Akan people, part of a larger group called the Nzima. Because he was born on Saturday, the infant was named Kwame. According to Akan custom, each baby receives a soul name depending on the day of the week of birth.

When Kwame was three, his mother took him to the town of Half Assini where his father, a goldsmith, had found work. It took three days to walk the fifty-mile distance along the dusty roads. His mother carried their belongings in a bundle on her head. When they stopped to sleep, they made a fire to keep wild animals away. "I had no fear of such things myself," he later wrote. "Like all small children I had complete confidence in my mother."

When he wrote his autobiography years later, Nkrumah remembered the deep bond between himself and his mother:

> Certainly my mother rarely denied me anything and doubtless I took advantage of this, but I believe that she tried not to make her affection too obvious because whenever she was serving our meals, she always gave me mine last.

However, his mother worried that he did not eat enough, and she placed bananas under his pillow in case he woke up hungry during the night.

Although Kwame was his mother's only child, his father had other wives, so Kwame grew up in the company of several half-brothers and sisters. Visiting relatives often arrived for long stays, swelling the family circle. Everyone shared in the work of tending the crops that provided most of their food. Though the family was poor, Kwame remembered only one time when he was envious of a neighbor—a child whose father had bought him a bicycle. Kwame's skills at dealing with others no doubt began within the bustling household.

His mother, a Roman Catholic convert, sent him to a one-room mission school. The first day, Kwame slipped out the door and ran home. But his mother was ambitious for her son to have an education and dragged him back. Seeing "that I had lost the battle," Kwame buckled down to work and, "To my surprise I soon found that I enjoyed my lessons." He even sold chickens so that he could help pay the school tuition and buy books.

After completing the eight-year course, Nkrumah stayed on as a teacher. Because he was so short, he had to stand on a box to write on the blackboard. One day a visitor appeared in his classroom—the head of a teacher-training college in the capital city of Accra. Impressed by the young teacher's ability, he invited Nkrumah to attend the college. Nkrumah accepted.

The big city, with its crowded streets and traffic, was bewildering to the country boy from Half Assini. He was often lonely. But a new influence appeared in his life—Kwegyir Aggrey, a man of immense vitality, charm, and charisma. Educated in the United States, Aggrey was vice principal of Achimota College, the first Gold Coast African ever to hold such a high position.

Aggrey planted radical new ideas in his students' minds. He told them that Africans were equal to the whites in all ways, but he advocated cooperation and understanding between the races. "You can play a tune of sorts," he would say, "on the white keys [of a piano] and you can play a tune of sorts on the black keys, but for harmony you must use both the black and white keys." Aggrey took a special interest in Nkrumah. He encouraged the young man to dream of studying abroad, where the schools could prepare him for a great role in life.

Nkrumah's years at Achimota were active ones. He took part in dramatics and sports and helped to form a student debate group. In the discussions, Nkrumah liked to take the position that most people disagreed with, to see if he could win the others over to his views. He often succeeded and recalled that his speaking ability "turned out to be my most valuable discovery."

After graduation in 1930, Nkrumah taught in Catholic schools. He soon became involved in the growing African nationalist movement. The Gold Coast had been a British colony since 1902. The British practiced indirect rule—they allowed the Africans to keep their traditional chiefs and leaders, but a small number of British officials held the real power. They met with the chiefs, giving them orders to pass on to the people.

For administrative convenience, the British and the other Europeans drew lines on the map, creating colonial nations. However, these "nations" often did not represent any real nationality. The "nation" called the Gold Coast, for example, included five major ethnic groups. Nkrumah's people, the Nzima, lived on both sides of the Tano River. But they were divided into French and British subjects when the Tano River became the boundary between the Gold Coast and a French colony, the Ivory Coast.

The British brought to the Gold Coast new, more efficient methods of mining gold and established plantations to grow cocoa. Yet most of the profits from these activities flowed to the British, rather than to the Africans. And Africans suffered the sting of racial prejudice, for even the humblest white person always made it clear that they were regarded as inferiors.

Nkrumah was stirred by the ideas of Nnamdi Azikwe, a Nigerian who established a newspaper in the Gold Coast. He wrote and published articles arguing for a rebirth of true nationalism in West Africa. Azikwe had been educated in the United States and urged Nkrumah to go there too. It was an echo of the dream

Kwegyir Aggrey had first instilled in the young man. Nkrumah decided that now was the time.

Nkrumah returned to Half Assini to bid farewell to his mother. As he stayed for a few days in her peaceful little village, she told him stories of his ancestors, "of the chief Aduku Addaie, the first of my forebears to settle in Nzima centuries ago."

Nkrumah began to fear entering a strange new world. He told his mother that he would stay behind if she wished. After looking at him for a few minutes, she said, "It cannot be helped. May God and your ancestors guide you." Nkrumah would not see her again for twelve years.

He spent the first of those years studying at Lincoln University, west of Philadelphia. It had opened its doors to other African students, including Nnamdi Azikwe. To pay for his tuition and food, he took whatever work he could find. During summer vacations, he peddled fish on the streets of Harlem in New York City. To avoid paying for a room to sleep in, he rode the subways all night, a trip that only cost a nickel.

During the ten years he lived in the United States, Nkrumah filled his mind with new ideas. He read unceasingly and listened to street-corner speakers who advocated full rights for African-Americans. Nkrumah was particularly impressed with the ideas of a Jamaican named Marcus Garvey. Garvey established organizations in the United States and the Caribbean islands to work for a free Africa. He believed that all black people would someday become part of one great free nation in Africa.

Even in the United States, Nkrumah experienced prejudice because of the color of his skin. In a bus station restaurant in Baltimore, he asked a waiter for a glass of water. The waiter rudely replied, "The place for you, my man, is the spittoon outside."

Though Nkrumah made many friends in the United States, his thoughts always returned to Africa. He later wrote, "Those years...were years of sorrow and loneliness, poverty and hard work." However, he added that he appreciated them "because the background they provided has helped me to form my philosophy of life and politics."

In 1945 Nkrumah sailed to Britain. Now thirty-eight years old, he was ready to begin his life's great work. With his own money, he published a pamphlet titled "Towards Colonial Freedom," in which he argued that Africans could only win independence by organizing and educating the people. He took a step toward accomplishing that goal by attending the Fifth Pan-African Congress in the city of Manchester.

The Pan-African Congress brought together blacks from all parts of the world. Nkrumah was thrilled to meet so many others who shared his ideas. He learned the techniques of organizing people into political parties, and how to take "positive action"—a term he would later give to his own policy. Positive action used nonviolent methods, such as strikes and boycotts, to force the colonial rulers to give up their hold on the country.

It was not long before Nkrumah would have a chance to try those ideas out in his homeland. After the end of World War II in 1945, the people of European colonies all over the world began to demand the freedom to govern themselves. The Gold Coast was no exception.

Seven thousand Africans from the Gold Coast had served in World War II on the Allied side. Returning home, these war veterans were not content to return to their roles as laborers for the colonial regime. The growing African middle class in the Gold Coast also wanted to have a greater voice in the government. A group of Africans formed an organization called the United Gold Coast Convention (UGCC). They were seeking an energetic organizer and decided to ask Nkrumah to take the job.

The thirty-eight-year-old Nkrumah left for the Gold Coast, eager to begin his work. But as he landed at the harbor at Takoradi in December 1947, he worried that the British police, knowing of his writings and political work, would arrest him on arrival. However, the immigration officer turned out to be an African. Checking Nkrumah's passport, he held it for a long time. Nkrumah feared the worst, but when the officer looked up, Nkrumah writes,

> He was looking at me in amazement, his eyes protruding from his head. Then his mouth moved slowly and he whispered softly: So *you* are Kwame Nkrumah!
> I nodded. The game, I felt, was up. He beckoned me to follow him and I did so. As soon as we had gone out of earshot of the other passengers and officials, his whole mannner changed. He shook my hand enthusiastically and told me how they—the Africans—had heard so much about me, that I was coming back to my country to help them, and how they had been wait-

ing anxiously for my arrival day after day. He told me to go on my way and that he would see to my papers.

Nkrumah proved to be a superb organizer with a flair for inspiring crowds. In his first speech he roused his listeners with a stirring challenge. "If in the past you have been sleeping, wake up now!" However, he found that the UGCC was a weaker organization than he had thought. Most of its members were in the cities, and they had modest goals. Nkrumah wanted to build a nation-wide movement—not just to obtain a voice in government, but to win complete freedom from Britain. Soon he was traveling about the countryside in a rattly old car, giving speeches and starting new branches of the UGCC. The British officials began to keep a sharp eye on him.

In 1948 the police in Accra blocked a protest march of African war veterans. In the scuffle, the police opened fire, killing two Africans. When the news spread, people rushed into the streets, attacking Europeans and looting their shops. Before the rioting ended the police had killed twenty-nine more Africans.

The British responded to the disturbance by arresting the leaders of the UGCC, including Nkrumah. In jail, the other leaders blamed Nkrumah for causing the trouble by his demands for total freedom. As he recalled,

> There appeared to be a general belief amongst them that the whole tragedy of our arrest and suffering was my fault, and

they began to make it plain that they regretted the day they had ever invited me.

After about six weeks Nkrumah and the others were released. But now he left the UGCC behind him and in June 1949 formed his own organization, the Convention People's Party (CPP). It called for "Self Government Now!" and put into effect his plan of "Positive Action." The disturbances that followed led to another prison stay for Nkrumah.

The British decided to cooperate with the "moderate" African leaders, the UGCC. The government announced elections for a new national legislature. For the first time, Africans would be allowed to vote for some of the members (but only a minority). In the elections of 1951, Nkrumah's party swept to victory over the UGCC candidates. Though Nkrumah himself was still in jail, he won election as a delegate. The British were forced to release him.

The new legislature elected Nkrumah as the Leader of Government Business. He showed his skill by taking strong measures to combat swollen-shoot disease, which threatened the cocoa trees that provided the colony's chief export crop. Yet he kept his eye on his main goal, which was to hasten the day of African self-rule. When he introduced a resolution calling for independence, it passed unanimously with white support.

The British recognized that they could no longer enforce their rule without widespread bloodshed. In 1956, the governor notified Nkrumah that independence would come on March 6 of the following year. The name chosen for the new country was Ghana—to commemorate the former great African empire. It marked the Africans' pride in their past and hope for the future.

Just after midnight on March 6, 1957, the British flag was lowered for the last time at Accra. Amidst the cheers of the thousands who had assembled, the red, green, and gold flag of Ghana was raised. All over the continent, others celebrated as well. A new era had begun for Africa.

Nkrumah dedicated himself to modernizing his country. He saw that the price of its cocoa exports fluctuated, producing cycles of prosperity and recession. So he urged farmers to plant other crops, such as bananas. When the cocoa prices declined, the farmers could survive by selling their other crops. Nkrumah's government sponsored the construction of factories to produce soap, cement, cooking utensils, and footwear. Ghana would no longer have to depend on foreign imports for the goods its people needed.

Knowing that many of his people could not read, he sent vans into the countryside to show movies that explained his programs. Nkrumah himself traveled throughout the country, meeting his people and winning their support. He built schools and hospitals, constructed roads to unite the nation, and improved the communications system that the British had built. A great dam on the Volta River provided hydroelectric power for the nation's new industries.

Nkrumah did not lose his dream of Pan-Africanism. A clause in Ghana's constitution allowed it to unite with other free African countries. As the leader of the first African country below the Sahara freed from colonial rule, he tirelessly worked for the freedom of others. In 1960 the French colonies of West Africa also won independence. Nkrumah soon united Ghana with the new country of Guinea, but the merger did not last. The lines that Europeans had drawn on the map of Africa proved hard to erase.

Unfortunately, Nkrumah started to flounder. He refused to allow any dissent to his rule, jailing critics of his policies. When the economy of Ghana declined in the early 1960s, Nkrumah's popularity fell with it. He responded by taking the powers of a dictator and outlawing all political parties but his own. He could not conceive of anyone but himself ruling the nation he had led to independence.

The inevitable followed. While Nkrumah was on an overseas trip in 1966, he received the news that Ghanian army officers had staged a coup and deposed him. He spent the last six years of his life as an exile in Guinea.

After his death, his body was returned to Ghana and displayed in the capital. Thousands of people passed by for a last look at the man who had led them to freedom. Throughout the country, flags were lowered to half-mast in mourning, and the radio stations broadcast his speeches.

At last, Nkrumah's body was taken back to his birthplace, Nkroful, for burial. His mother, gray and frail, still lived there, and the townspeople kept a vigil outside her home all night. As his body was lowered into the ground, his mother said, "He was the salt that seasoned Ghana and Africa." Despite his mistakes as a ruler, he will always be remembered as the first modern African to lead his nation to independence.

CHAPTER 10

A WRITER FROM TWO WORLDS—
WOLE SOYINKA

Each day little Wole watched as his father crossed out the date on the calendar for 1938. Wole was impatiently looking forward to the thirteenth day of July—his fourth birthday. Wole had already told his best friends about the great event, promising them a wonderful party. As the days passed, the importance of the birthday grew ever larger in his imagination, so that he was sure everyone else in his family was preparing for it.

When the great day arrived, Wole brought a dozen classmates home from school. They settled down to wait for the food and drinks to appear. But Wole gradually noticed that no one else was at home. He peeped into the kitchen and was surprised to find no pancakes ready, no pot of special *jollof* rice. He checked the calendar again and saw the date was right. Well, he thought, perhaps mother had been delayed at her shop in the market.

Indeed, his mother soon arrived, and seemed surprised to find the house full of children. "Now Wole," she said, "tell me, what have your friends come for?" Wole was puzzled. "We've come to eat Birthday," he replied. She gently chided Wole. He should have told her that his friends were coming so she could have prepared for a party.

It was a lesson to Wole. People did not always see things the same way he did. That was to be true throughout his life.

Even so, the party was a success. His mother quickly made some goodies, and the children entertained each other with songs. When Wole sang, his best friend Osiki drummed on the table with such skill that Wole's mother asked jokingly whether he had been drumming for the yearly masquerade. Osiki caused a sensation when he said yes. His family compound had its own mask for the annual festival of the *egungun*. The egungun were spirits of the dead, sometimes very scary ones. It was said that bad egungun could strike a person with illness. Violent ones had to be tied up with ropes. But Wole had watched the egungun parading past his house, and noticed that many of them knew his name and even joked with him.

Wole and the other children gathered around Osiki, asking him questions. "Are you actually there when the egungun emerges from the bottom of the earth?" asked Wole.

"Any of us can watch. As long as you are male of course. Women musn't come near," replied Osiki. Wole was excited and insisted that he must attend the next festival. His mother, however, was horrified and forbade him to go.

Wole pressed Osaki further. "Can I come back as an egungun if I die?" he asked. His friend's response was disappointing. "I've never heard of any Christian becoming an egungun," he said firmly.

Wole Soyinka spent his childhood in two worlds—one rich in African folklore and wisdom, the other influenced by Christianity and European ideas. Later, when he became one of Africa's most famous writers, he would combine both parts of his heritage.

Wole Soyinka grew up in the small Yoruba town of Abeokuta in western Nigeria. His father Ayo was the headmaster of a Christian school, and young Wole absorbed his love of books. Before he was three, Wole followed his older sister to the primary school and demanded to be taught. He was put with the youngest children and allowed to stay.

Eniola, his mother, was so devout in her faith that Wole wryly called her the "Wild Christian" in his affectionate book about his childhood. She could be tender and kind but was quick to apply a stick to any of her children who misbehaved.

Wole's uncle taught him the Yoruba lore. He took Wole to the woods to collect mushrooms, snails, and firewood. The forest was alive with spirits, and young Wole learned that supernatural forces affected their daily lives. Down the street lived a girl who was believed to be *abiku* (part of both the spirit world and the living) because she often fainted.

In the evenings Wole's family listened to the radio, which brought ominous news from Europe. World War II was about to break out. Even in Abeokuta the villagers worried about this terrible German dictator, Hitler. An old warrior patrolled the street with his magical gourd and stick, on guard for an attack by the Nazis.

Yet Wole's family also resented their status as colonial subjects of Great Britain. When Wole was ten, he took part in a protest against the high taxes they had to pay to the British government. When the British refused their petitions to lower the taxes, the women of Abeokuta took matters in their own hands. They called for a closing of all the markets, traditionally run by women, in protest. The "Wild Christian" was one of the ringleaders in the effort, and Wole acted as a courier. Squads of women confiscated the goods of anyone who did not cooperate in the protest.

Wole went to the local school till he was eighteen and then attended the University of Ibadan, about forty-five miles from his home. During his two years as a student, Wole started to write stories and poems. Some of them appeared in a magazine called *Black Orpheus*. In 1954 a scholarship enabled him to attend the University of Leeds, in Britain, where he studied world literature.

After graduating with honors, he accepted an invitation to join the Royal Court Theatre in London. Two of his plays were produced to rave reviews. He might have been tempted to remain in Britain, but he knew his roots were at home. As he wrote at this time, "Untouched I float, upon the crest of an alien, white society."

Soyinka returned to Nigeria in 1959, where he worked in the theater in Ibadan. Excitement was in the air as the colony prepared for independence the following year. Soyinka was asked to write a play for the occasion. He created *A Dance of the Forest*, a drama centering on a tribal religious ceremony in which the spirits of the dead are called to glorify the past. Soyinka had not forgotten his uncle's teachings, but he put his own wry spin on them—in the play, when the spirits appear, they are not the glorious ancestors that were expected. The people are afraid of them and refuse to welcome them. This was Soyinka's way of saying that modern Nigerians have turned their backs on their true past.

During the next few years, Soyinka traveled through Nigeria, studying traditional folk dramas that were still presented in villages. This gave him a chance to experience the great variety of cultures within his nation. The three main groups were the Muslim Hausa, the Christian Ibo, and Soyinka's own Yoruba people. Nigeria included the people who had produced the great brass sculptures of Benin. In the early twentieth century, the British had combined several of their colonies around the Niger River into a larger colony they called Nigeria.

The study of folk customs and stories enriched Wole's writing. He sought to create a new kind of literature—one that blended African traditions with modern forms and points of view. His job as head of the drama department at the University of Ibadan enabled him to continue writing. But the quiet life of a university professor was not to be his fate. He was concerned not only with the past, but also with Nigeria's turbulent present.

In 1965 Soyinka published his first novel, *The Interpreters*. Set in Nigeria's capital city, Lagos, it deals with the dilemma of Africans who have received a modern education—like himself. They are caught between the traditional ways of their people and the appeal of modern society in a fast-changing Nigeria. In *The Interpreters* Soyinka also expressed his concerns about the growing political corruption in his new nation. As in Ghana, the African leaders who took control after independence did not always rule wisely or well.

Soyinka developed this idea more fully in his next play, called *Kongi's Harvest*. Kongi is a cruel and arrogant dictator in an imaginary African country. The action of the play revolves around Kongi's attempts to force a traditional *oba*, or king, to perform the harvest festival rites—but with Kongi as the god. *Kongi's Harvest* was presented at the First Festival of Negro Arts at Dakar, the capital of Senegal. From all over Africa, musicians, dancers, writers, and scholars converged on Dakar for a celebration of the continent's cultures.

Soyinka's career became overshadowed by political events in Nigeria. Conflict between its different ethnic groups was about to erupt into civil war. After independence, the government was controlled by the Muslim Hausa. The Ibo people, in the eastern part of the country, resented their lack of power. In May 1967 the Ibos seceded to form an independent nation called Biafra. The Nigerian government sent troops to quell the rebellion.

At the time, Soyinka was in the United States, planning a movie of *Kongi's Harvest* with his friend, the American actor Ossie Davis. Soyinka hurried home, hoping that he could help bring about a peaceful settlement to the civil war. On August 4 he wrote an article in a Nigerian newspaper, appealing for a halt to the fighting. "There will be no victory for anyone in the present conflict," he wrote, "only a repetition of human material wastage and a superficial control that must one day blow up in our faces and blow the country to pieces."

Three days later he met with the Biafran leader Odumegwu Ojukwa, hoping to persuade him to negotiate a peaceful settlement. On August 17 the Nigerian government arrested Soyinka. Without announcing any charges against him, and with no trial, the government sent him to Kaduna prison in northern Nigeria.

He spent most of the next two years in solitary confinement. Soyinka endured the worst possible punishment for a writer—cut off from any human contact to refresh his spirit, not allowed any books to occupy his mind. Yet he could not be silenced. In his loneliness and rage, Soyinka wrote parts of a play and poetry on scraps of paper like the backs of cigarette packs. One poem, smuggled out of prison, he called "Live Burial." It begins by describing his cell:

> Sixteen paces
> By twenty-three. They hold
> Siege against humanity
> And truth

Though alone, he was not forgotten. Writers in other nations took up his cause and demanded his freedom. The government had hoped to silence him, but instead added to his fame. His plays were performed in the United States and Britain, bringing more attention to his unjust detention. Under pressure, the government finally released him in October 1959. Soyinka soon made it clear that his spirit had not been crushed. One of the Nigerian government's slogans in its war against Biafra was, "To keep Nigeria one is a task that must be done." Soyinka called a news conference after his release and declared, "To keep Nigeria one justice must be done."

Reunited with his family, Soyinka returned to the University of Ibadan. A few months later, the Nigerian civil war came to its bloody conclusion with the defeat of Biafra. More than a million Ibos had died in the struggle, many from starvation.

Soyinka brought a troupe of Nigerian actors to the United States to perform the play he had written in prison, *Madmen and Specialists*. Though the play is set "nowhere in particular," it describes a tyrannical and corrupt government, and audiences guessed what had inspired it.

In 1981 he published one of his most popular works, *Aké, the Years of Childhood*. This affectionate recollection ends in the author's twelfth year, as the Nigerians' desire for independence is stirring. When readers demanded that he continue his life story, Soyinka responded in a way that was typically contrary to what others expected. In 1989 he published a book that took his family history farther into the past. *Ìsarà: A Voyage Around Essay* was a loving account of his father's life and times. (His father's initials were S.A., and because he loved reading so much, his son called him "Essay" as a pun.)

In 1986 Soyinka received the highest honor that a writer can receive—the Nobel Prize for Literature. He was the first writer from Africa to win the coveted prize. His career, however, is far from over. Soyinka's main love continues to be the theater. Though many of his plays deal with Nigerian folklore and modern problems, audiences all over the world enjoy them. Soyinka has attained his goal of creating African literature that is universal in its appeal.

CHAPTER 11

THE RUNNING POLICEMAN—
KIPCHOGE KEINO

It was a bright summer day in Mexico City in 1968. Kipchoge Keino of Kenya placed his feet in the starting blocks and waited for the starter's gun to fire. Next to him were seven of the fastest men in the world. The 1500-meter race in the Olympic Games was about to begin.

Keino's chances of winning a medal seemed slim. He was suffering from severe stomach cramps, due to a gall bladder infection that would require an operation soon after the Olympics. His condition was made worse by the exhausting series of races he had already run. His performance had been disappointing.

When Keino lined up for his last chance at a gold medal, the experts shook their heads. He might have had a chance of winning the 1500, they said, if he had not used up his strength in the two longer races. What's more, the favored runner in the 1500 was a man Keino had faced before, but never beaten. Jim Ryun of Kansas held the world's record time for this distance, and the experts predicted that he would win again.

Keino seemed to have only one thing going for him. The air in Mexico City was thin because Mexico City is more than 7,000 feet above sea level. Athletes found that they tired more easily than usual, and the winning times in the long races reflected this. However, Keino was not worried because he had trained in his homeland at altitudes of over 5,000 feet.

Keino had planned a risky strategy for the race. Jim Ryun was known for his "kick," or ability to accelerate with strength at the ending of a race. Keino planned to neutralize this advantage by building such a large lead that Ryun could not catch him.

Bang! went the starter's gun, and the eight runners leaped out of the starting blocks. Keino's teammate from Kenya, Ben Jipcho, took off like a rocket to lead the way. Jipcho established a killingly fast pace for the first 400 meters. Then Keino took the lead, flying past the 800-meter mark in the unheard-of time of 1:55.3.

Ryun was far back, but he, along with almost everyone else, believed that Keino was squandering his strength too early. With two laps to go, Ryun went into his "kick," and began to catch up. The crowd held its breath. Would Keino be able to keep up such a pace or would he run out of power? Amazingly, Keino didn't slow down. Ryun moved up but got no closer than twelve meters when he gave out. Kipchoge won by twenty meters. His final time was three minutes, 34.9 seconds, an Olympic record that would not be broken for sixteen years. It was also nearly two seconds faster than Keino himself had ever run the 1500 meters.

Kipchoge stood proudly atop the victory stand, wearing the gold medal around his neck and listening to the band play the national anthem of Kenya. The crowd was used to that anthem by now. Keino's gold medal was the third won by members of Kenya's track team at the 1968 Olympics. They were the first Olympic gold medals Kenya had ever won.

Kipchoge Keino was born on January 17, 1940, near Kipsano, a village in what was then the British colony of Kenya. He grew up with his three sisters on a farm. His job was tending to the family cattle. "My father did not like it when I went to school," he said, "because then I could not watch the cattle."

Kipchoge ran barefoot to school and back—six miles each way. He liked to play soccer. Because his family was too poor to buy a regular ball, he used an old tennis ball or a homemade ball of rope. Sports equipment was an unheard-of luxury in Kipchoge's village.

He gave up soccer to concentrate on running, because he clearly showed great talent and speed. He felt it was not good to concentrate on two sports, so he chose his best one. Running required no equipment, and he could train any time he wanted to. He thought all he had to do was run fast. However, when he met world-class runners for the first time, he found that was a mistake.

At eighteen, Keino became a policeman, but he kept up his running. His talent began to draw attention, and when he was twenty-two, he was chosen to compete in the Commonwealth Games in Perth, Australia. Runners from all parts of the British

Empire would be competing in the track and field events there.

The trip was a thrilling experience for the young Kenyan. It was not just his first trip outside his homeland, but the first time he ever rode in an airplane. The trip was a long one, and he changed planes several times. "I saw the differences of people," he said, "how they looked and acted." Asians, Africans, Canadians, Australians—so many people in the British Empire that he had seen before only in the pages of his geography book.

However, the competition at Perth showed Keino that his running style had a weakness. He just ran at the same pace throughout the race—all out as fast as he could from start to finish. He did not know how to conserve his strength and "kick" at the end. Years later, Keino smilingly described the race to a journalist:

> I got to be way ahead in the race....I was half a lap ahead, and then was 200 yards ahead and we came to the last lap. We came to the stretch, and then, shhh, one is by me. Shhh, two is by me. Shhh, three comes. I am thinking they are all coming by me. Four, five, six. Shh, shhh. They are all sprinting. I was annoyed. I could do nothing.

He thought about the race, and realized what he had done wrong. He ran too fast at the beginning, but he had another problem. His natural stride was very long. Each step he took was about eight feet. This meant that he had less power than runners with shorter strides. He spent too much time "coasting" in the air.

Back home Keino began to practice. He shortened his stride to six feet, and began to develop a "kick." He learned how to develop a strategy for each race. When there was a "rabbit," or fast starter in a race, Keino should not try to keep up with him, but to conserve his strength for the end.

At this time, the most famous runner in Kenya was Wilson Kiprugut, a sergeant in the army. He was burning up the tracks of the world and setting records. Kiprugut was so famous that in December 1963, it was he who was chosen to lower the British flag and raise the new flag of an independent Kenya. The country cheered as Kiprigut brought home a bronze from the Tokyo Olympics in 1964—the first Olympic medal any Kenyan had ever won.

Keino also competed at Tokyo, running in the 5,000 and 1500-meter races. His best finish was a fifth in the longer race. But he was still young, and the next year, his career exploded. He set new world records in the 3,000 and 5,000 meters, and he ran the mile in three minutes, 54.3 seconds—a little more than a second over the world record. That was also the year when Keino came up against his greatest rival, the American Jim Ryun. Time after time, they met in the 1500 meters, the closest metric race to the mile. Ryun always won, but racing against Keino seemed to push the American to his best speed. Both looked forward to the 1968 Olympics.

In Kenya runners were superstars. A street in Mombasa, Kenya's second-largest city, was named Kipchoge Keino Street. Even so, the government could not afford to pay for the luxurious training facilities and internationally known coaches that athletes from other countries enjoyed. Younger runners did not even have shoes. Though Keino became one of his country's most beloved figures, he still trained alone, running six miles a day along hilly, dusty roads with only himself as a coach.

Keino kept his job in the police department. He liked the work and it gave him time to train. His promotion to chief inspector enabled him to move into a new two-bedroom home with a garden. There, he displayed trophies from his many track victories. Among the photographs on the walls were many showing him with Jomo Kenyatta, the leader who won independence for Kenya.

Now president of Kenya, Kenyatta often invited Keino to parties at the presidential palace. Kenyatta said to him, "When you go off to other places to run, and you win, you win for yourself but, you are Kipchoge of Kenya." He ran for Kenya's glory.

Thus, when Keino prepared to leave for the Mexico City Olympics, Kenyans dreamed of seeing him run in the three major middle-distance races—the 10,000, 5,000, and 1500 meters—and winning all three. Kipchoge realistically thought it might be better to concentrate on one. But a journalist in Nairobi, Kenya's capital city, publicly warned that Keino might lose the opportunity to be a three gold-medal winner. Keino replied: "It is easy for you to say, 'Run all three, Kipchoge,' You will sit and write while I run."

Yet Keino gave in and entered all three events when he went to Mexico City with a very strong team of Kenyan athletes. Doctors advised him not to try the grueling schedule, for they worried about his violent stomach pains.

His first event had been the 10,000-meter race. Keino had been up with the leaders with only two laps to go, when he doubled

over in pain and fell to the side of the track. Stretcher-bearers came to carry him away, but the proud Kenyan struggled to his feet and finished the race. His only consolation was that the winner had been his fellow Kenyan, Naftali Temu. Kenya finally had a gold medal, but it was not Keino's. Four days later he ran in the 5,000 meters, taking second place and a silver medal. That was not enough. He had to win the 1500 or return home in disgrace.

The day of the race, Keino almost didn't make it to the stadium in time. The taxi in which he was riding had become stuck in traffic. Impatiently, Keino got out and jogged the last mile to the stadium. That was hardly good preparation for competing against the world's fastest runners.

Yet Keino would not be denied the victory he had practiced so long to win. When he telephoned home to tell his family, his joy increased. That very day, his wife had given birth to their third daughter. In honor of her father's triumph, she was given the name Olympia.

Returning home, the runners found a mob of people waiting to greet them at the airport. All over Kenya, people rejoiced. The Kenyans' success showed that the original spirit of the Olympics was still alive. Even without the special training that wealthy countries provided their athletes, a true amateur could win.

"MUSIC IS A TYPE OF MAGIC"—
MIRIAM MAKEBA AND
JOSEPH SHABALALA

The soccer stadium in Zimbabwe's capital city, Harare, was rocking in February 1987. Twenty thousand people, including Zimbabwe's Prime Minister, stomped and hollered to the beat of the music. The occasion was the kickoff concert for the world tour of American pop singer Paul Simon's *Graceland* album.

Among the crowd were thousands of spectators who had traveled by bus from neighboring South Africa. The concert was, in fact, a celebration of South Africans' own music. For Simon had assembled the album from songs composed by performers in little night clubs and dance halls in the black ghettoes of South African cities. On stage with Simon in Zimbabwe were South Africa's most famous singers—Miriam Makeba and Joseph Shabalala.

In many ways the Graceland concert was a return to the source of the world's most popular music. Africans wrenched from their homeland as slaves brought with them the rhythms and musical styles of Africa. In the New World this music developed in different ways. Jazz, blues, rock, and rap music from the United States, reggae and salsa from the Caribbean, and samba from Brazil are only some of the many kinds of modern pop music with African roots. Through radio, records, and tapes, this music spread back to Africa, where it blares from radios and boom boxes in cities throughout the continent. The popular sounds influenced the new music being created today by South African songwriters like Shabalala. And now that music, too, was gaining international fame through *Graceland*.

The Graceland tour could not perform in South Africa itself, because the United Nations (UN) had called for a cultural boycott of the country. The reason was South Africa's policy of *apartheid*, or

racial separation, which the world community had condemned. Although black Africans form more than eighty percent of South Africa's population, until recently they had been deprived of basic human rights by the white minority government. Paul Simon agreed to abide by the UN policy. Miriam Makeba told the crowd, "I hope and wish sometime we will be able to invite Paul Simon to Johannesburg in a free South Africa."

It had been thirty years since Miriam Makeba brought South African music to the attention of the world. In 1957 she skyrocketed into the American popular music scene. The beauty of her silky voice delighted audiences, who were fascinated by the sharp clicks that were part of her Xhosa language. A Xhosa warrior song that she introduced later became a hit as "The Lion Sleeps Tonight."

Miriam was born March 4, 1932, in Johannesburg. Her father was a Xhosa, and her mother a member of the Swazi tribe. Times were tough for the family, for those were the years of the world-wide economic depression.

When Miriam was five, her father died. Her mother took a job caring for the children of a white family in Johannesburg. Miriam was sent to live with her grandmother in Pretoria. But Miriam did not feel alone, for the Xhosas have a strong family tradition. Within her grandmother's compound lived twenty-one children. Each family had built a house from bricks made of mud, and everyone shared the work.

"No little girl is supposed to sleep until sunrise," Miriam's mother told her, and by the time the adults were up, the children had swept the courtyard, made a fire, and brought water from the well. Carrying a four-gallon pail of water on her head made Miriam feel grown up. Then everyone sat down to dip from the "big bowl of cornmeal with fried tomatoes and onions and, if we are lucky, meat sauce."

Terror came at night, when the white police made their random raids on black communities. One night Miriam was awakened by banging on the door. Everyone had to get up and show their passbooks. In South Africa all blacks had to have a pass which identified where they could live. Anyone found outside their authorized location was arrested. Miriam was terrified when the police struck her uncle when he did not produce his passbook quickly enough. But no one protested, for everyone knew of people who had been taken away by the police, never to be seen again.

Cruel as this treatment was, it became worse when Miriam was sixteen. A new South African government made *apartheid* its official policy. Many blacks were sent to "homelands" in distant parts of the country. Those who were needed to work in the cities were forced to live in crowded townships outside the areas reserved for white homes. Black children were given only enough education to enable them to serve whites.

The government banned protests, political meetings, even books and newspapers criticizing the system. Miriam found her own way of coping with racism—music. She loved singing in the school choir and listening to jazz and blues records from the United States. Miriam discovered that

> music is a type of magic. Music can do all sorts of things. It can make sad people happy. It can make dull people sit up and pay attention. I know what it does to me. Music gets deep inside me and starts to shake things up. I begin to squirm. My lips turn into a smile and my hands begin to clap against one another. My body moves. It is as if I am possessed.

When one of her cousins formed a band, he asked Miriam to perform as the lead singer. Miriam's voice attracted the attention of the Manhattan Brothers, one of the most popular groups in South Africa. From then on her career went nowhere but up. Her records made her popular all over the country, and people came up to her in the street to tell her how much they loved her music.

However, fame, for blacks, also had its price. Police cars often stopped Miriam and the Manhattan Brothers on their way home from a concert. Blacks needed a special stamp in their passbooks to be out at night. Though the group always took care to have the proper permissions, sometimes the police locked them up anyway. "There are times," wrote Miriam, "when each African wonders how much longer we can stand living the way we do....There is only so much anger, resentment, pain, and fear that can build up in a person before there is an explosion."

In 1954 Miriam met someone who was working "to keep that explosion from happening." She sang at a special performance for the African National Congress. One of its leaders was Nelson Mandela, who would become a worldwide symbol of the fight against apartheid. After the concert Mandela—like her, a Xhosa—told her how much he liked her singing; she was too shy to look at him, and mumbled thanks before rushing off.

The next year was a momentous one, both for Mandela and for Miriam. The African National Congress issued a Freedom Charter that declared, "South Africa belongs to all who live in it, black and white." The huge crowd that gathered at the reading of the charter were all arrested. From that time, the South African government tried ceaselessly to stamp out the Congress and persecute its leaders.

Miriam was one of the lucky few South Africans who would gain her personal freedom. An American filmmaker came to South Africa and put her in his movie *Come Back, Africa*. When it appeared, she received an invitation to perform on an American television show. In 1957 she left South Africa, not knowing that she would not see it again for thirty-two years.

In the United States Miriam found that audiences were entranced by the warrior chants and love songs that she had learned while growing up. African Americans, seeing the natural way she wore her hair, began to take up this "Afro" style.

Thrilled with the freedom she had in the United States, Miriam stayed to record albums and to sing on television. But her performances made the South African government uncomfortable, for in her music she expressed her feelings about living under apartheid. Here, no one could stop her from speaking freely.

In 1960 a little place called Sharpeville also showed the world what South Africa was like. A crowd of blacks had gathered there for a protest march. Police arrived and began to fire into the line of marchers, killing sixty-nine people, including ten children. Letters from home told Miriam that two of her uncles were among those who died in the Sharpeville Massacre. "I weep and weep," Miriam wrote, "and in my bitterness I can feel something hard, a resolve, form inside."

Later that year she received worse news. Her mother had died. Miriam went to the South African embassy to obtain a visa to fly home for the funeral. Instead, when she presented her passport, an official stamped it "INVALID." The South African government did not want her to return. She was too famous, too much in love with freedom, too "dangerous."

"And so," she wrote, "I became a spokesperson for my people." Unable to return to her friends and relatives, she raised her voice in support of them. She spoke before the United Nations, urging it to boycott trade with South Africa. She sang at colleges throughout the United States, bearing witness to her people's struggle for freedom.

Makeba's music reflected the pain of her homeland—a country where the government itself actively supported racism. "I look at an ant," she wrote,

> and I see myself: a native South African, endowed by nature with a strength much greater than my size so I might cope with the weight of racism that crushes my spirit. I look at a bird and I see myself: a native South African, soaring above the injustices of apartheid on wings of pride, the pride of a beautiful people.

Her people's struggle was only beginning. In 1962 Nelson Mandela was sentenced to life in prison. But Makeba was among those who would not allow the world to forget him. She wrote to his wife Winnie, offering her support. Makeba continued to sing and speak out, and the world listened.

She traveled throughout Africa, acquainting herself with the rich musical culture of each country. She added new songs to her performances. Throughout the world, she became known not only as a Xhosa, not only as a South African, but as an African. In 1963 she sang for the independence celebration in Kenya. She made a new home in the African nation of Guinea.

In 1987 Makeba burst back onto the international scene at the Graceland concert in Harare. There she met Joseph Shabalala for the first time. Unlike her, Shabalala had spent all his life under apartheid. Yet like Miriam, he had freed his spirit through music.

When Shabalala was a boy in the late 1940s, he sang to ward off loneliness while he herded his family's sheep and cattle. As he looked at the blue skies, melodies and songs would come to him as if by magic.

Joseph's father was a Zulu migrant worker, away from his family for eleven months of the year. This was a common plight for black males in South Africa. Although the government needed black workers in the cities and mines, it refused to allow them to bring their families with them. The Shabalala family lived in a mud hut in the rural district of Ladysmith. Life was hard, and the six

children in the family had very little to look forward to.

When he was a teenager, Shabalala went to Durban to find work. There, living in a shabby hostel in a black township with other Zulu workers, he found others who liked to sing. To ease their loneliness and sorrow, the workers gathered in clubs on weekends, listening to amateur groups that competed against each other for small prizes. The style of township singing was called *ischatamiyah*, which means "walking softly on the toes."

With some of his friends, Shabalala formed a group and they started to enter the fierce Saturday night competitions. The group belted out labor union anthems and pop songs that they had heard on the radio. They learned to sing loud, because the clubs had no microphones and the crowds were noisy.

But Shabalala was not satisfied. Something about the music was missing. One night, he had a dream. He saw a chorus of children, floating between the stage and the sky. "At first," he said, "I thought God just wanted me to be happy, but as time went on I caught the tune and copied down their actions. Unfortunately I didn't understand their strange language so I made up my own words."

In 1973 Shabalala started a new group with three of his brothers and cousins. Because none of them could read music, Joseph had to teach each one how to sing their parts. He named the group Ladysmith Black Mambazo—the black axe of Ladysmith. The axe is a symbol of power. When the group sang at clubs, they announced themselves with: "Here are the boys of the axe! Beware! Here are the boys of the axe!" In a short time, they became so popular that they won every competition they entered. A record company signed them up, and their first album zoomed to the top of the charts. They made enough money to quit their jobs and concentrate on music full time.

Much of Shabalala's music was inspired by his Christian faith. He became a preacher in his local church, and he has said that the songs he composes are gifts from God. But his music also comes from Zulu work songs, which people invented to ease their toil in fields and mines. In the group's performances, Shabalala's gentle tenor leads the way by calling out questions that the deep bass voices of the chorus answer. The "call and response" gives way to swelling harmonies that set audiences to clapping.

In 1984 Shabalala was astonished to receive a phone call from the world-famous American singer, Paul Simon. Simon asked him to bring the group to make an album in London. That was the beginning of *Graceland*, which became a gigantic international hit.

Shabalala, however, will never have to become an exile like Miriam Makeba. South Africa has begun to change. Pressure from the other nations of the world caused its government to begin to abandon apartheid. In 1990 Nelson Mandela was released from prison. Now gray-haired, his face lined from twenty-eight years in jail, he showed that he had not lost his energy or his determination to bring about a society in which all people are equal. As head of the African National Congress, he began negotiations with the white government. Among his first demands was the return of all those who had been exiled because of their political protests.

And so, in June 1990, Miriam Makeba finally came home. Though her music had been banned from South African airwaves for years, a crowd greeted her at the airport. She led them in singing *Nkosi Sikeleli Afrika* ("God Bless Africa"), the anthem of the African National Congress.

The following April she gave two concerts in a Johannesburg park. The audience included both whites and blacks, making it an event that would have been banned only a few years before. At last, Makeba said, she could sing her songs where she did not have to explain what they meant.

G L O S S A R Y

Abiku: In Nigeria, a being that was part of both the spirit world and the living world.

Abolitionist: A person who advocated a ban on slavery.

Abuna: A bishop of the Ethiopian Christian church.

Amon: God of the sun in the religion of Egypt and Kush.

Apartheid: "Apartness." The South African government's policy of separating the racial groups of the country.

Askia: A word that originally meant "thief." Muhammad the Great, ruler of the Songhay Empire, took it as his title because he seized power from his predecessor.

Barracoon: A warehouse or holding pen where slaves were kept before being sold or shipped.

Catalan Atlas: A map made by the European Abraham Cresque in 1375. It contains a drawing of Mansa Musa of the empire of Mali, and calls him "the richest and most noble king in all the land."

Dynasty: A line of rulers belonging to one family.

Egungun: In Nigeria, a spirit of the dead; could be dangerous or benign.

Geber: In Ethiopia, a feast of celebration.

Griot: An African oral historian, who memorizes and passes down the lore and history of his people from generation to generation. Also called a remembrancer.

Hajj: The pilgrimage to Mecca that each Muslim is required to make once in a lifetime.

Ischatamiyah: Literally, "walking softly on the toes." A name for a popular style of singing in the nightclubs of South Africa's black townships.

Islam: A religion founded by an Arab merchant, Muhammad, in the seventh century A.D. Its followers spread it to many parts of Africa and other continents.

Katama: In Ethiopia, a large residence or estate. The katama of Queen Taitu became the site of the modern nation of Addis Ababa.

Koran: The holy book of the religion of Islam. In Islamic countries, it is used as a guide to policy and law.

Ladino: A slave who was born in the New World. After the importation of new slaves from Africa was outlawed in the 19th century, it was still legal to buy and sell Ladinos.

Litham: The blue cotton mask, with eye-slits, that was worn by the Tuareg people of the Sahara Desert region.

Mansa: The title of the emperors of Mali.

Middle Passage: The journey that brought Africans to the New World as slaves.

Muezzin: A prayer-leader of Islam, who calls the people to prayer in the mosques five times a day.

Negus nagast: Literally, "king of kings." The title for the emperor of Ethiopia.

Ngola: The title of the rulers of Ndongo. The name for today's nation of Angola comes from it.

Oba: The title of the rulers of Benin.

Obelisk: A high, thin pillar used as a monument.

Oni: The title of the rulers of Ife.

Polygamy: The cultural practice of a man's being allowed to take more than one wife.

Positive Action: Kwame Nkrumah's methods of protesting British colonial rule in Africa. Included strikes and boycotts.

Ras: A title of the kings of Ethiopia.

Remembrancer: See Griot.

Sahara: Arabic for "wilderness." Name given to the desert that divides north Africa from the southern two-thirds of the continent.

Shammas: In Ethiopia, a long gown with embroidered hems.

Uraeus: Coiled snake that was the symbol of the power of Egypt's pharaohs.

B I B L I O G R A P H Y

Addison, John, *Traditional Africa*, St. Paul, MN: Greenhaven Press, 1980.

Balandier, Georges, *Daily Life in the Kingdom of the Kongo*, New York: Pantheon Books, 1968.

Bloom, Pamela, "Ladysmith Black Mambazo," *Musician*, July, 1987.

Boahen, A. Adu, et al., *The Horizon History of Africa*, New York: American Heritage Publishing Co., 1971.

Breasted, James Henry, *A History of Egypt*, New York: Bantam Books, 1967.

Clark, Leon E., ed., *Through African Eyes*, v. 1, New York: ACITE Books, 1988.

Clarke, John Henrik, "African Warrior Queens," *Journal of African Civilizations*, Vol. 6, No. 1, April, 1984.

Clarke, John Henrik, "Ahmed Baba, a Scholar of Old Africa," *Negro History Bulletin*, Vol. 41, No. 6, Nov.-Dec., 1978.

Davidson, Basil, *The African Genius*, Boston: Atlantic Monthly Press, 1969.

Davidson, Basil, *African Kingdoms*, New York: Time-Life Books, 1966.

Davidson, Basil, *Black Star: A View of the Life and Times of Kwame Nkrumah*, New York: Praeger, 1973.

Davidson, Basil, *The Lost Cities of Africa*, Boston: Little, Brown, & Co., 1959.

Egharevba, Jacob, *A Short History of Benin*, 4th ed., Ibadan, Nigeria: Ibadan University Press, 1968.

Erlmann, Veit, "A Conversation with Joseph Shabalala," *World of Music Magazine*, 11/1/1989.

Fradin, Dennis Brindell, *Ethiopia*, Chicago: Children's Press, 1988.

Gillon, Werner, *A Short History of African Art*, New York: Penguin Books, 1984.

Hallett, Robin, *Africa to 1875*, Ann Arbor, MI: University of Michigan Press, 1970.

Hodgkin, Thomas, *Nigerian Perspectives*, 2nd ed., New York: Oxford University Press, 1975.

Isichei, Elizabeth, *History of West Africa Since 1800*, New York: African Publishing Company, 1977.

Jackson, John G., *Introduction to African Civilizations*, Secaucus, NJ: The Citadel Press, 1970.

July, Robert W., *A History of the African People*, New York: Scribner's, 1974.

Kendall, Timothy, "Kingdom of Kush," *National Geographic*, Vol. 178, No. 5, Nov. 1990.

Kenworthy, Leonard S. and Ferrari, Erma, *Leaders of New Nations*, Garden City, NY: Doubleday, 1968.

Lamb, David, *The Africans*, New York: Vintage Books, 1987.

Makeba, Miriam, *Makeba: My Story*, New York: Plume Books, 1989.

Marcus, Harold G., *The Life and Times of Menelik II*, Oxford: Clarendon Press, 1975.

Murphy, E. Jefferson, *History of African Civilization*, New York: Dell, 1972.

Nkrumah, Kwame, *The Autobiography of Kwame Nkrumah*, New York: International Publishers, 1957.

Oliver, Roland, and Fagan, Brian M., *Africa in the Iron Age*, Cambridge: Cambridge University Press, 1975.

Osae, T.A., Nwabara, S.N., and Odunsi, A.T.O., *A Short History of West Africa*, New York: Hill & Wang, 1973.

Rogers, J.A., *World's Great Men of Color*, v. 1., New York: Collier Books, 1972.

Sale, J. Kirk, *The Land and People of Ghana*, rev. ed., Philadelphia: J.B. Lippincott, 1952.

Segal, Ronald, *African Profiles*, Baltimore: Penguin Books, 1962.

Shinnie, Margaret, *Ancient African Kingdoms*, New York: New American Library, 1965.

Soyinka, Wole, *Ake', the Years of Childhood*, New York: Vintage Books, 1983.

Soyinka, Wole, *A Shuttle in the Crypt*, New York: Hill & Wang, 1972.

Thompson, Robert Farris, *Flash of the Spirit*, New York: Vintage Books, 1984.

Tuesday Magazine, editors of, *Black Heroes in World History*, New York: Bantam Books, 1969.

Underwood, John, "Lost Laughter," *Sports Illustrated*, 9/30/1968.

Weaver, Kenneth F., "The Search for Our Ancestors," *National Geographic*, vol. 168, no. 5, 11/1985, p. 560.

Weigall, Arthur, *Personalities of Antiquity*, Freeport, NY: Books for Libraries Press, 1969.

S O U R C E S

Chapter 1: Piankhy
pages 6-7: "Hermopolis threw herself..." Jackson, John G., Introduction of African Civilizations, p. 113.
page 9: "While you were yet..." Kendall, Timothy, "Kingdom of Kush," p. 124.
page 10: "Do not stop..." Weigall, Arthur, Personalities of Antiquity, p. 188.
page 11: "I have [made] the seal...." Rogers, J.A., World's Great Men of Color, p. 92.
page 12: "Listen to what I did!..." Weigall, op. cit, p. 187.

Chapter 2: Ezana and Lalibela
pages 16-17: "And as I have sent..." Murphy, E. Jefferson, History of African Civilization, pp. 51-52.
page 17: "would do a cubit's work..." Ibid., p. 55.

Chapter 3: Mansa Musa
page 23: "This man spread upon Cairo..." Addison, John, Traditional Africa, p. 27.
page 24: "The small number..." Ibid., p. 27.

Chapter 4: Ahmed Baba
pages 25-26: "people of gentle and cheerful..." Addison, op. cit, pp. 27-28.
page 28: "was a man of goodness..." Hodgkin, Thomas, Nigerian Perspectives, p. 117.
All other quotations in this chapter from Clarke, John Henrik, "Ahmed Baba, a Scholar of Old Africa"

Chapter 5: Euware the Great
page 32: "The people..." Hodgkin, op. cit., p. 82.
page 36: Quotations from Dutch visitors, Davidson, Basil, African Kingdoms, p. 104
All other quotations in this chapter from Egharevba, Jacob, A Short History of Benin.

Chapter 6: Ann Nzinga
page 40: "It is not fitting..." Rogers, op. cit., p. 248.
page 43: "a cunning and prudent..." Clarke, John Henrik, "African Queens"

Chapter 7: Cinque
page 51: "fellow men...seized..." Tuesday Magazine editors, Black Heroes in World History, pp. 108-109.

Chapter 8: Menelik II and Taitu

page 52: "stoutly built..." Rogers, op. cit., p. 378.

page 54: "I have arrived...." Fradin, Dennis Brindell, Ethiopia, p. 107.

page 55: "Do not let the Europeans..." Boahen, A. Adu, et al., The Horizon History of Africa, v. 2, p. 429.

page 56: Dialogue between Menelik and Italian ambassador, Rogers, J.A., op. cit., p. 373.

page 56: "I am a woman..." Marcus, Harold G., The Life and Times of Menelik II, p. 130.

page 56: "permit our integrity..." Rogers, op. cit., pp. 373374.

Chapter 9: Kwame Nkrumah

page 59: "You have opened my eyes..." Nkrumah, Kwame, The Autobiography of Kwame Nkrumah, p. 48.

page 61: "Certainly my mother..." Ibid., p. 8.

page 64: "He was looking at me..." Ibid., p. 66
    pages 65-66: "There appeared to be..." Ibid., p. 82.

page 67: "He was the salt..." Davidson, Basil, Black Star, p. 207.

Chapter 10: Wole Soyinka

pages 69-70: Quotes from birthday party, Soyinka, Wole, Aké, the Years of Childhood, pp. 30-32.

page 73: "Sixteen paces..." Soyinka, Wole, A Shuttle in the Crypt, p. 60.

Chapter 11: Kipchoge Keino

page 76: "My father did not like it..." Underwood, John, "Lost Laughter," p. 96.

page 78: "I got to be way ahead..." Ibid., p. 96.

page 79: "When you go off..." Ibid., p. 97.

page 79: "It is easy..." Ibid., p. 96

Chapter 12: Miriam Makeba and Joseph Shabalala

pages 81-83: Quotes from Simon and Makeba at Harare, Newsweek, 2/23/87.

page 83: "big bowl..." Makeba, Miriam, Makeba: My Story, pp. 9-10.

page 84: "music is a type of magic...." Ibid., p. 15.

page 84: "There are times..." Ibid., pp. 54-55.

page 85: "I weep..." Ibid., p. 97.

page 86: "I look at an ant..." Ibid., p. 1.

page 87: "At first I thought God..." Bloom, Pamela, "Ladysmith Black Mambazo," p. 19.

INDEX

Abeokuta, 70, 71
Accra, 61, 65
Achimota College, 61, 62
Adams, John Quincy, 51
Addis Ababa, 55, 58
Adowa, Battle of, 56, 57
Adulis, 13, 16, 17
Aduku Addaie, 63
Aedesius, 13, 15
African National Congress, 84, 85, 88
Aggrey, Kwegyir, 61, 62, 63
Ahmad el-Mansour, 29, 30, 31
Ahmed Baba, 26-31
Amistad (ship), 45, 47, 48, 49, 50
Amon, 8-12
Angola, 38, 40, 41
Ankober, 52
apartheid, 81
Arawan, 26
Askia the Great, See Muhammad, Askia
Axum, 13, 15, 16, 17, 56
Azikwe, Nnamdi, 62, 63
Benin, 32, 33, 34, 37, 72
Biafra, 72, 74
Bini, 32, 34, 36, 37
Boromeda, 56
Britain, 48, 54, 55, 62, 63, 66, 71, 74, 76, 78

Cairo, Egypt, 23, 25
Catalan Atlas, 23, 25
Christianity, 15, 17, 18, 42, 43, 44
Cinque (Joseph), 45-51
Convention People's Party, 66
Cresque, Abraham, 23
Davis, Ossie, 72
Egharevba, Jacob, 37
Egypt, 6, 8, 9, 10, 11, 12, 13, 55
Ella Amida, 15
Eritrea, 55
Ethiopia, 15, 16, 17, 18, 52-58
Euware the Great, 34, 36, 37
Eweka, 32
Ewere, 36, 37
Ezana, 15, 16, 17
Frumentius, 13, 15
Fungi, 43
Gao, 24, 26, 31
Garvey, Marcus, 63
Ghana, Empire of, 21, 22, 23
Ghana (modern country), 21, 59, 66, 67
Gold Coast, 59, 61, 62, 64
Guinea, 21, 67, 86
Haile Selassie, 57
Haiti, 45, 48
Half Assini, 59, 61, 63
Harare, Zimbabwe, 81, 86
Hausa, 71, 72
Heliopolis, 11
Hermopolis, 6, 10
Hill of Barkal, 8, 12

Ibadan, University of, 71, 72, 74
Ibn Battuta, 24
Ibos, 71, 72, 74
Ife, 32, 33, 34
Iguegha, 32, 33, 34
India, 12, 13
Islam, 17, 19, 22, 23
Italy, 55
Ivory Coast, 62
Jagas, 40
Jipcho, Ben, 75
Johannesburg, 83, 88
Judson, A.T., 50
Kangaba, 22
Kashta, 9, 10
Keino, Kipchoge, 75-80
Kenya, 4, 75, 76, 78, 80, 86
Kenyatta, Jomo, 79
Kiprugut, Wilson, 78
Kipsano, 76
Kongo, 40
Koran, 24, 29, 30, 31
Kumbi Saleh, 22
Kush, 6, 8, 9, 12
Ladysmith Black Mombazo, 87
Lagos, 72
Lalibela, King, 17-18
Lalibela (city), 18
Leakey, Louis, 4
Leakey, Mary, 4
Leo X, Pope, 25
Leo Africanus, 25, 26
Liberia, 58
Luanda, 38, 40, 41
Makeba, Miriam, 81, 83-88
Mali, Empire of, 19, 21, 22, 24, 33

Mali (modern country), 21, 31
Mandela, Nelson, 84, 85, 86, 88
Mandela, Winnie, 86
Mani, 47
Mansa Musa, See Musa
Marrakesh, 29, 30, 31
Matamba, 43, 44
Mauritania, 21
Mecca, 17, 19, 22, 23, 24, 25, 28
Mediterranean Sea, 5, 12, 13
Memphis, Egypt, 10
Mendi, 47
Menelik (I), 15, 54
Menelik II (Sahle Mariam), 52-58
Meroe, 12
Mexico City, 75, 79
Mombasa, Kenya, 79
Morocco, 21, 22, 29, 30
Muhammad (founder of Islam), 17, 30
Muhammad, Askia, 26, 28, 29
Musa (Mansa), 19, 21, 22, 23, 24, 28
Mussolini, Benito, 57
Nairobi, Kenya, 79
Namlot, 6
Napata, 8, 9, 12
Ndongo, 38, 40
Nefru-ka-Kashta, 12
Ngoli Bbondi, 41
Niane, 19
Niger River, 28, 72
Nigeria, 33, 36, 70, 71, 72, 73, 74
Nkroful, 59, 67

Nkrumah, Kwame, 59-67
Nok culture, 33
Nzima, 59, 62
Nzinga, Ann, 38-44
Oduduwa, 32
Ojukwa, Odumegwu, 73
Ogun, See Euware
Oguola, 32
Olduvai Gorge, 4
Oyoyo, 36
Pan-Africanism, 64, 67
Piankhy, 6-12, 16
Portuguese, 37, 38, 40, 41, 42, 43, 44
Ras Dashen, 17
Roha, 17, 18
Ruiz, Don Jose, 48, 49
Ryun, Jim, 75, 76, 79
Saba, 15
Saba, Queen of, 15, 54
Sahara Desert, 5, 19, 21, 25, 29
Sankore, University of, 28, 31
Sasso, 22
Senegal, 72
Shabaka, 12
Shabalala, Joseph, 81, 86-88
Sharpeville, South Africa, 85
Shoa, 52, 54
Sierra Leone, 47
Simon, Paul, 81, 83, 88
Solomon, King, 15, 54
Solomonid Dynasty, 15
Songhay, Empire of, 24, 26, 28, 29, 31, 33

South Africa, 81, 83, 85, 88
Soyinka, Ayo, 70, 74
Soyinka, Eniola, 69, 70
Soyinka, Wole, 69-74
Spain, 48, 49
Sudan, 55
Suleiman, 24
Sundiata, 22
Sunni Ali, 26
Swazi, 83
Taitu, 52-58
Takoradi, 64
Tano River, 62
Tappan, Lewis, 50
Tem-Bon-Dumba, 43
Temu, Naftali, 80
Theodore (Tewodros), 54
Tigre, 54, 56
Timbuktu, 24, 25, 26, 28, 29, 31
Tuaregs, 19, 21
Tutankhamen, 9
Ubi, 36, 37
Umberto, King, 56
United Gold Coast Convention, 64, 65, 66
United States, 48, 49, 50, 59, 61, 62, 63, 72, 74, 81, 85
Van Buren, Martin, 50
Volta River, 67
Xhosas, 83, 85, 86
Yohannes, 54, 55
Yoruba, 70, 71
Zagwe Dynasty, 17, 18
Zimbabwe, 81
Zulus, 86, 87, 88

MEDORA COMM SCHOOL LIBRARY

MEDORA COMM. SCHOOL LIBRARY